ABOUT THE AUTHOR

Brian John Rance is a retired university-built environment academic and, more recently, Assistant Director of the Estates and Facilities Department at Birmingham City University. He holds a diploma in Town Planning from Oxford Brookes University and a master's degree in Social Science from Birmingham University. He has two daughters and lives with his partner in Kings Heath in South Birmingham. He was born in 1949 in Woolwich and grew up in Eltham and Welling in south-east London, attending Westwood Secondary School and Bexley Grammar School. He spent his youth exploring the Kent countryside as far as Romney Marsh on the channel coast. He has produced four previous books concerned with Kent and East Sussex and has walked thousands of miles in the process. This book, his fifth, and closer to home, records a 150-mile circumnavigation of the West Midlands conurbation.

A MIDLAND MEANDER

A CIRCULAR WALK AROUND THE WEST MIDLANDS

BRIAN J. RANCE

The Book Guild Ltd

First published in Great Britain in 2023 by
The Book Guild Ltd
Unit E2 Airfield Business Park,
Harrison Road, Market Harborough,
Leicestershire. LE16 7UL
Tel: 0116 2792299
www.bookguild.co.uk
Email: info@bookguild.co.uk
Twitter: @bookguild

Copyright © 2023 Brian J. Rance

The right of Brian J. Rance to be identified as the author of this
work has been asserted by them in accordance with the
Copyright, Design and Patents Act 1988.

All rights reserved. No part of this publication may be
reproduced, transmitted, or stored in a retrieval system, in any form or by any means,
without permission in writing from the publisher, nor be otherwise circulated in
any form of binding or cover other than that in which it is published and without
a similar condition being imposed on the subsequent purchaser.

Typeset in 12pt Minion Pro

Printed and bound by CPI Group (UK) Ltd, Croydon, CR0 4YY

ISBN 978 1 91535 222 4

British Library Cataloguing in Publication Data.
A catalogue record for this book is available from the British Library.

Contents

Acknowledgements	ix
Introduction	xi
Full Circular Route Map	xiv
Chapter 1: Alvechurch to Kinver	1
Chapter 2: Kinver to Brewood	35
Chapter 3: Brewood to Tamworth	66
Chapter 4: Tamworth to Alvechurch	87
Appendices	120
Copyright Acknowledgements	124

Acknowledgements

I am, once again, indebted to Allan Buxton, who has produced the excellent route maps which accompany this, my fifth book. As before, I would like to thank all those people I have met on my travels who have provided material for this walking companion guidebook around the West Midlands. Finally, I would like to thank my daughters Jessica and Eleanor (known as Ellie) for their encouragement and my long-suffering partner Wendy for her patience and support in this ambitious project.

Introduction

What I like about solitary walking in this country is the sense of relying on one's own physical and mental resources. I know it's not like walking in the Amazon or trekking through Africa but nevertheless, out in the country, in the fresh air with a map, is very satisfying. I enjoy navigating with old-style maps, a skill which is, I imagine, now in short supply, since the rise of mobile phones and Global Positioning Systems. It feels like an achievement just to get from one place to another, finding the way, getting out of a tight corner, reorientating oneself when lost. However, a mobile phone has proved to be very useful in working out where one actually is and is always there in case one had need to ring for help, an occurrence I have never (yet), thankfully, had to resort to. It also helps if the phone is charged and there is enough money to pay for taxis. Now in my seventies, I am content to take my rambles at a more leisurely pace. I feel entitled to do this now since, when I was younger, in my fifties and sixties, I would cover, day after day, prodigious distances, glorifying in the achievement and recorded in my first four books, concerned with the wonderful counties of Kent and East Sussex. Now I take it easy, walking at a more leisurely pace.

I read John Hillaby's 1960's eccentric romp from Land's End to John o'Groats, which he started at the age of fifty, and I realised that my own efforts, started at the same age, were in fact comparable, both in terms of the distances covered and the style of writing. However, he was, in my view, slightly more inclined to get in tight corners, was content to sleep rough and, curiously, eschewed the wearing of decent walking boots. I have always worn tight-fitting walking boots and as a consequence have never suffered from blisters. In my rambles I never had to sleep in a ditch, or under a hedge, but, like him, called into as many pubs as possible. I have concluded that my efforts, although not quite as adventurous, are seriously underappreciated at the current time.

And then of course there are the more recent best-selling books of Robert Macfarland, who has written lucidly about the experiences of walking. Reading his books, I was encouraged to try to emulate this style, making a lot more of the pleasures of rambling. He also reintroduced me to the poems of Edward Thomas, for which I am extremely grateful. My favourite poem of his is *'Over the Hills'*, which contains a number of evocative lines that sum up my feelings perfectly. Edward Thomas (1878–1917) was an English poet and essayist, born in London of Welsh parents and educated at Oxford University. On the outbreak of the First World War, he enlisted as a private and had received his commission as a second lieutenant when he was killed at Arras at the age of thirty-nine. What a terrible waste! Like many men of my generation, I feel it is a great privilege that I have never had to fight in a war, much as I believe they are very rarely justified.

Although Macfarland, like me, has walked thousands of miles, and he eulogises about maps, there is not a single route map in his discourse recorded in his books, an omission that I find disappointing because I like looking at maps. He describes the geological map of the British Isles as a 'document of great beauty', in his book entitled *The Old Ways*. I also have the same map permanently upon my study wall and would enthusiastically concur with his sentiments. My fascination with the rocks under our feet was engendered at school while studying for a geology O level in the 1960s, at the splendid Westwood Secondary school in Welling, south-east London, a distinctly unusual subject at the time. I was taught by a Mr. Osbourne, a wonderful teacher of the subject to whom I am, no doubt, posthumously, immensely grateful. I have, from time to time, on this circular ramble, because of my abiding interest in the subject, referred to the rocks under my feet and the geomorphological processes that have shaped the landscape.

This, my fifth book, concerns a 150-mile circumnavigation of the West Midlands conurbation undertaken over two Covid-19-ravaged years. This walk skirts around the built-up area of my adopted city of Birmingham and the composite towns and cities of the conurbation. Solitary walking, and walking in general, during this time has proved to be one of the safest activities anyone could imagine, a pastime I would thoroughly recommend. Now this epic journey is complete, and given that walking is part of my DNA, I will have to give serious consideration to my next rambling challenge.

Chapter One
Alvechurch to Kinver

I decided to start my next adventure from Alvechurch, a large village in North Worcestershire to the south of Birmingham. I drove down to the car park tucked around the back of The Red Lion Inn, which was amazingly free, managing to grab the last vacant car parking space. I imagine that most of the parked cars belonged to commuters using the nearby train station to access Birmingham city centre. Changing into walking gear, I strolled down to the heart of the village and turned right up Bear Hill, past the church, along a narrow road flanked by old, Victorian-painted, black-and-white dwellings. Alvechurch is really a very attractive village, set in the headwaters of the River Arrow, which, flowing south, joins the Worcestershire Avon in Bidford, but proximity to Birmingham, where I live, probably means I take it more for granted than anything else. Rising all the time, just over the railway, I reached the Worcester and Birmingham Canal and headed south towards Tardebigge. Across the canal, as one might expect, there was a

Alvechurch: Junction of Bear Hill & Red Lion Street © Lee J. Andrews

A MIDLAND MEANDER

Map 01: Alvechurch to Bromsgrove

large marina, housing many colourful narrowboats and industrious boatyard activities bedecked with cranes and pulleys.

I struck out along the towpath, on a canal elevated precariously above the surrounding countryside. There were a few boats on the water but relatively little other activity. Setting off along this canal, I realised that this would be the first of many such encounters, since the Midland plateau is crisscrossed by this landscape feature, culminating in Birmingham, the centre of the Midlands canal network. This occurrence gives rise to that oft-quoted assertion that Birmingham has more canals than Venice. As I plodded along the level, gloomy canal, I was trying to convince myself that the monotonous scene in this section was not too boring.

After about a mile or so of easy walking, I hit the first tunnel and had to take the gradually rising footpath, which once would have taken all the carthorses over the hill while boatmen legged it through the tunnel. At the top of the footpath I crossed over the unseen canal below and was diverted across the Worcestershire countryside, the original path parallel to the canal being blocked. After scrambling through woods and across arable fields, I came back to the open canal, but having been twisted round and finding myself on the other side of the canal, I did wonder whether I had simply gone round in a circle. I thought I might even be in danger of heading back to Alvechurch, but after consulting with a group of amiable young lads – released from school during summer holidays and amusing themselves by swinging out across the water by a stout rope secured to a tree up the bank – they confirmed I was indeed headed south to Tardebigge. I was for a fleeting moment tempted to ask them whether I could have a go, swinging out over the water, but thought better of it.

I carried on along the towpath, around some sharp bends in the canal hugging the contours, before reaching another canal boat marina prefacing the second tunnel on this stretch. As the tunnel dived underground, I took the parallel narrow lane southwards, coming up to the B4096, the original road from Redditch to Bromsgrove. Then by taking the short footpath opposite, still the surrogate towpath, I came down by steep steps to the newer, faster dual carriageway, carving mercilessly through the landscape, the A448, connecting the same two Worcestershire towns. I crossed the road carefully by an elaborate dog-legged footpath in the central reservation. I thought the least those responsible for the project could have decently done was to provide a footbridge over the road.

Leaving the route of the canal, I strolled along the B4184 into the dispersed ancient village of Tardebigge. I crossed back under the big road and, to my dismay, found that the eponymously named pub, which I was aiming for, was closed for refurbishment. I carried on, wondering how I would be able to get back to Alvechurch since the buses on this road only ferried between Bromsgrove and Redditch, going nowhere near Alvechurch. I went inside the nearby craft centre and frequented the café there where the ladies serving kindly ordered me a taxi. The taxi driver joked about me having visited the nearby Hewell Grange HM Young Offender Institution which had recently experienced serious rioting. Returning to Alvechurch, I popped into The Red Lion for a lunchtime drink, celebrating the fact that I had started another long-distance ramble, this time around the West Midlands conurbation. I wondered how long it should be until I would be sitting once again in this pub, celebrating the completion of my ambitious project.

Resuming my journey from the craft centre at Tardebigge – where I was hoping to have breakfast in the café in recognition of the kindness previously proffered and, to be frank, to assuage my early morning hunger – I found, unfortunately, that it didn't open until ten o'clock. The weather was cloudy but, more importantly, dry. I struck out past the Tardebigge pub, which was now irritatingly open for business, and passed back under the fast road from Redditch to Bromsgrove by a dark, functional tunnel. I took the small lane which led to the church and local school. The school was nestled in the churchyard, an adjacency which demonstrated the religious origins of this Church of England school. This juxtaposition also reflects the close entanglement of this particular religious denomination in the United Kingdom State, an anachronism that some may feel is unacceptable in a multi-ethnic society. Seriously though, I feel very strongly that the identification of nation states with particular religions is the cause of much modern, and historical, strife around the world. Personally, like the arrangement in France, or the supposed constitutional provision in India, I would much prefer that all state-sponsored education was secular in nature.

Strolling through the churchyard, I searched for a footpath down to the Birmingham and Worcester Canal. From the back of the churchyard, tripping down through the extension filling up with newly dug, flower-strewn graves, there were fabulous views across the canal and of the rising ground towards the Malvern Hills and Welsh hills in the distance. Straight ahead, in the foreground, I could see the Lickey Hills and Barnt Green and, to my left, the sprawling town of Bromsgrove. I passed through the graveyard extension, over a stile and through a field of sheep back down to the Worcester and Birmingham Canal.

I hit the canal by a quaint lockkeeper's cottage guarding the top lock of the Tardebigge flight; a massive flight of thirty narrow

Tardebigge Top Lock © Rudi Winter

locks leading down off the Midland plateau. The Midland plateau is composed of a layer of Mercia mudstone, formerly known as Keuper marl, overlying Bunter sandstone laid down in desert conditions in the Triassic geological period, when Birmingham was located in the tropics east of the present Caribbean Sea. The fact that we are now graced with these rocks is due to the relentless progress of continental drift, a process that takes place in unfathomable geological time. To illustrate the point, I understand that the Atlantic Ocean gets wider every year by about the same distance as our fingernails grow each year.

Loitering by the top lock, I met three elderly fellows out from Birmingham girding their loins for an ambitious trek down the canal to Worcester. By way of encouragement, I suggested to them that they would not encounter many hills on the way; indeed, I imagine it is all downhill. Wishing them well, I strode on down, winding my way along the carefully manicured curving towpath, under warm, elegant, brick-built bridges. I imagine the lockkeepers, formerly employed by the British Waterways Board, would have as one of their duties mowing the grass verges of the canal. Even though the signs still proclaimed British Waterways ownership, this government department has now been abolished, with its charge, that is looking after two thousand miles of historic waterways, being transferred to the Canal and River Trust, a charity set up in 2012. I passed by the adjacent Tardebigge reservoir designed to top up water in the canal when required by a connecting concrete shoot construction. It is perhaps not widely realised that canals have to be topped up with water from time to time when they have leaked, and indeed, it is possible to pull the plug to let the water out altogether when serious reconstruction is required.

Just after the reservoir, I left this attractive stretch of canal by crossing over another charming humpbacked bridge and picked up the small lane to Stoke Cross, which, until it reached the first house, was no more than a dirt track. It was a lovely day for walking and from the lane there are great views across to Bromsgrove dominated by its striking church spire which, as one would expect, can be seen for miles around. In time, I came to the crossroads which is Stoke

Cross, a junction of three colourfully named lanes: Grimley Lane, Dusthouse Lane and Walnut Lane. I proceeded along Walnut Lane, picking up the Monarch's Way, searching for a footpath across fields to the B4184 and Aston Fields on the outskirts of Bromsgrove.

This would not be the first encounter with the Monarch's Way, a 625-mile long-distance footpath, in my perambulation northwards through Worcestershire and South Staffordshire. It was created to commemorate the escape route of Charles II after defeat at the battle of Worcester in 1651 in the English Civil War. Initially, the king fled northwards from Worcester via Chaddesley Corbett, Stourbridge and Womborne, as far north as Boscobel and Madeley on the River Severn, but he turned tail to return south through the now West Midlands conurbation to Stratford. Thereafter, the king worked his way into the West Country before returning along the south coast to Brighton, thus accounting for the exceptional length of this footpath. Whilst I have no intention of walking this protracted escape route, I would, on this journey, toy with the first abortive northern meander when the deposed king was seeking assistance from royalist catholic-supporting gentry of North Worcestershire and South Staffordshire.

Finding the footpath I was looking for, I left the lane. The Monarch's Way along this stretch was well articulated with efficient metal kissing gates. I passed through fields blessed with sturdy oak trees marching in straight lines, no doubt marking former field boundaries. Approaching the outskirts of Bromsgrove, in the vicinity of Aston Fields, I passed a large, well-appointed sports ground devoted to the playing of rugby, a game which I have enjoyed watching but regrettably never played, since the schools I attended in south-east London only provided for football and cricket. I have to admit that I have often fantasised about playing scrum half, given that when I was younger, I had a good turn of speed over the first couple of yards. Coming up onto the main B4184, I crossed over the main Birmingham-to-Worcester railway line.

In Aston Fields, once a separate village from Bromsgrove, I popped into a good-looking café for a late breakfast at quarter to eleven. I had to wait a long time to get anything to eat in the very busy café, and although I chose to sit out on the edge, I felt I was very much regarded in a slightly suspicious manner. I'm sure that some customers arrived after me and were served first, but maybe that was acceptable, them being locals and well known to the proprietors. I might be wrong but sporting a rucksack and dressed in scruffy walking gear seems to engender in persons a sense that I might be a vagrant and up to no good, or maybe a sensitivity to so-called small-town immigrant issues.

I passed through a lively local centre in Aston Fields with a railway station, a pub and a Travelodge, and a posh coffee shop, giving the place a somewhat separate identity from Bromsgrove. I noticed a Polish bistro on my way across to the A38, the Bromsgrove bypass, feeling again that look of distaste from local residents. I don't think I was imagining it. Crossing over the ring road, I passed the Bromsgrove town sign confirming my surmise that Aston Fields was once a separate community now conjoined, and I wondered whether locals still regarded Aston Fields as a separate place. I slogged up the road alongside a small stream, between local schools and the extensive Charford council estate, and reached the main A38 road through Bromsgrove just as the rain set in. I didn't have far to go to the centre of Bromsgrove, and the rain was only light, which was lucky because my wet gear was still in my golf bag. I did, however, put on my cap to keep my head dry.

I passed the grand entrance to the very posh Bromsgrove school, one of the oldest public schools in England founded in 1553, and continued north through the scruffy approach to the town centre from this direction. The roadside consisted of a disharmonious mixture of old terraced cottages, newer blocks of flats and wholesale warehouse premises. Looking up I could see the Lickey Hills looming large on the skyline. When I reached the pub, pretentiously called Ye Old Black Cross, I popped in for a well-deserved pint. This was the very pub that I had stayed in many years ago on a previous walk from Birmingham to Chepstow down the Severn Valley. Sitting in the downtrodden front bar, I admired the sturdy old oak beams in the ceiling. I checked with the landlord that the pub used to offer accommodation, and he confirmed it did, and would, after refurbishment, offer it again in the future. After a statutory visit to the toilets, I noted that the pub footprint was very deep, which, together with the relatively narrow frontage, confirmed the medieval origins of the plot.

I continued on up the high street, into the pedestrianised section, and sampled the second pub, The Red Lion. I gained a very similar impression, of a very old, unimproved drinking establishment, graced by single elderly men this lunchtime, some of whom had caught the bus out from Birmingham, using their bus passes to pretend that they were still alive and kicking. Behind the bar paying appropriate respect was a large picture of A. E. Housman, a local lad who wrote the collection of popular bucolic poems called '*A Shropshire Lad*' in 1896. He attended the nearby Bromsgrove school and was a renowned scholar at Oxford University, evidently writing his verse without ever visiting Shropshire, using good-sounding place names to enhance his poems. He described the Shropshire countryside, some of which I would visit on my clockwise perambulation around the West Midlands, poetically as 'the land of lost content'. I resisted the temptation to enquire of the inmates whether they were familiar with his works. Carrying on, past a grand statue to the great man sculpted by one Kenneth Potts, I popped into the third pub, The Queens Head, at the top of the high street, another very old, dusty pub. Here, sitting at the bar, I was regaled by a noisy group of tattooed day trippers out from Birmingham, getting drunk this lunchtime, evidently escaping from a turbulent block of flats in the inner city.

Bromsgrove: Statue of A. E. Housman
© Philip Halling

Bromsgrove

> *A scruffy high street*
> *Housman stands tall*
> *Thinking of Shropshire*
> *Not visited at all*
> *Lurking under Lickey Hills.*

I reflected on the generally downtrodden feel of Bromsgrove town centre, with its ageing pedestrianised high street. In the 2018 referendum, along with many small towns up and down the country, Bromsgrove voted to leave the European Union when immigration issues formed a central plank of the leave campaign, although, curiously, Brexiteers now prefer not to mention it. Wondering whether there was a large immigrant population in Bromsgrove, I strolled back to the bus station. I considered catching a bus into Birmingham but thought better of it, knowing how long the journey would take, winding its way back through Catshill and Rubery. I frequented the very commodious toilets by the terminus before grabbing a taxi to take me speedily back to Birmingham.

Returning to Bromsgrove a few weeks later, I strolled out from the bus station, down the ring road towards the magnificent parish church. I observed another small stream running beside the ring road, constituting one of the headwaters of the River Salwarpe, which joins the River Severn after flowing through Droitwich. Turning left onto the A448, I passed out of the town. I took the Monarch's Way again through the very large and well-appointed Sanders Park to the next road. Crossing over another small stream, I found a quiet lane opposite, colourfully named, Timberhonger Lane. I pressed on under the M5 motorway, up the lane and over a steep little ridge at 101 metres. Descending off the ridge between high hedges, the sound of the motorway began to dissipate. At one point, the view opened up and in front of me I could see right over to the well-wooded Abberley Hill and, to my left, I could see the distinctive profile of the

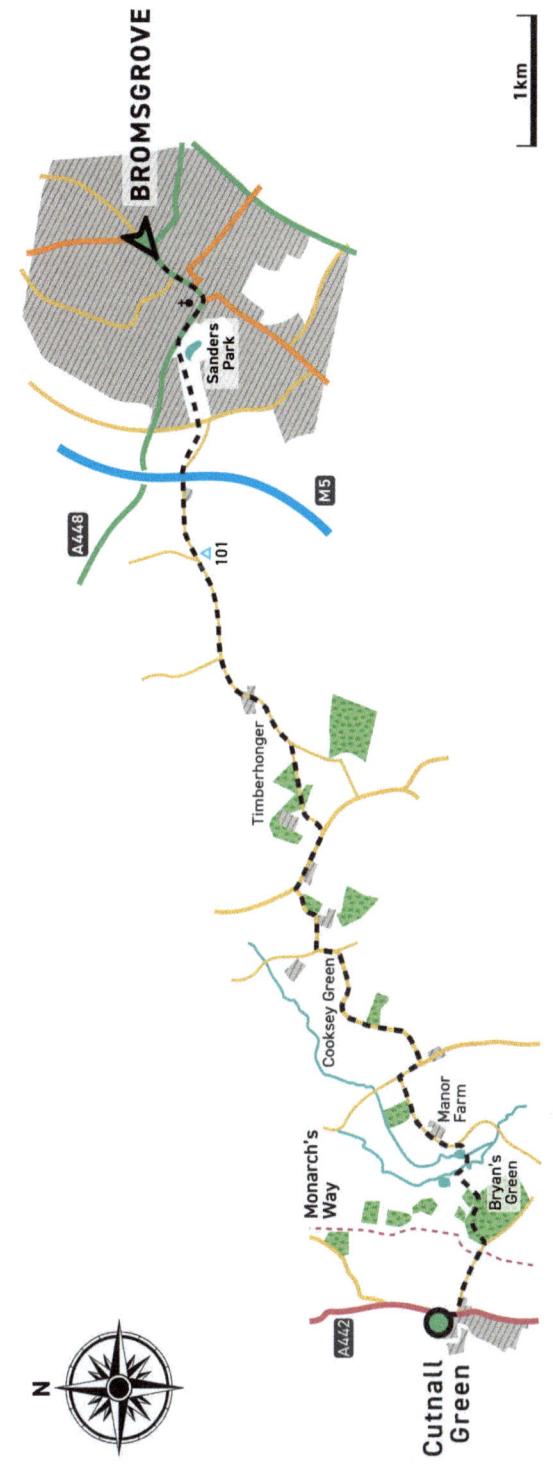

Malvern Hills which, observed from the right angle, reminds me of a recumbent Easter Island statue. Further round still, I could see the disused radio masts at Wychbold and the spa town of Droitwich.

As I proceeded ever westwards, picking blackberries from the hedgerow, the clouds rolled in, threatening rain. Crossing the undulating terrain, I passed through the scattered hamlet of Timberhonger. In Timberhonger Lane, I saw evidence of badger activity and an arresting swirl of swifts. Coming to a bigger north/south lane, I turned north for a short distance in the light rain, light enough not to bother with wet gear, which was a good job as I had left said items, once again, in my golf bag. I carried on along the winding Cooksey Green Lane, passing through a basically rural landscape dotted with pleasant, cared-for houses, demonstrating the affluence of the owners. Leaning on a farm gate and looking northwards across arable farmland, I could see both the Clent and Lickey Hills in the distance, forming a major watershed between rivers flowing northwards over the Midland plateau to the Trent and those flowing southwards through the country I was traversing to the Severn.

I strolled on through the hamlet of Cooksey Green, reflecting on the seminal events happening in Parliament on this day, namely the passing of beneficial legislation which would hopefully prevent the UK leaving the EU without a sensible deal. I noted a sign pinned to a garden fence which encouraged people to report incidents of hare coursing, a particularly barbaric pastime and clearly a problem in this vicinity. Failing to find a footpath to my right, I came to a field sporting nine massive carthorses who thudded over to me for a stroke. After a dog-leg, I entered the unfenced and gated lane to Manor Farm, which felt more like a stately home, with its carefully tended verges. I chased and scattered hordes of quail down the lane in front of me which, when they could not outpace me, dived into the hedgerow for cover. I pondered on the question, what use were quail? I'd heard of quails' eggs but could think of no other purpose for the wild bird, but maybe that is because I don't habitually frequent expensive restaurants. To the back of the impressively large and grand Manor Farm, I came across a field of pretty goats and then a paddock with four large shaggy sheep, which, by the way, were prepared to stand their ground, and the impressively large assembly of undercarriage body parts, I guess, were prized breeding rams.

At the corner of the lane, I decided to take a footpath to Bryan's Green. I ambled down to two small streams that, coalescing, flowed down to the centre of Droitwich, crossing over by a well-marked footpath with metal kissing gates. But then, as often happens, the way became unclear and, walking out of the valley, I ended up, probably illegally, picking my way around the edge of an orchard. The orchard was graced by an elaborate framework supporting netting that could be rolled down to protect the crop when required, which I thought might be cherries. Finding my way up to the lane in Bryan's Green, I turned west towards Cutnall Green. I crossed over the Monarch's Way again and came up to the main A442, the Droitwich to Kidderminster Road. Reaching The Chequers pub, a large roadhouse in Cutnall Green, I naturally popped in for something to eat and drink, joining the well-to-do, retired leisured classes out for lunch. Although I perceived the usual disapproving glances, I was extremely well looked after by the young bar staff, one of whom kindly ordered a taxi for me. I returned to Bromsgrove and caught a bus back into Birmingham.

Continuing my perambulation a few weeks later, I caught a taxi back from Bromsgrove to Cutnall Green to resume my escapade. The driver only wanted to talk about his favourite football team, namely Aston Villa, also a team I have adopted since my long residence in the West Midlands. When I worked at the university in Perry Barr, I could see Villa Park, set in grounds formerly belonging to Aston Hall, from my office window. I did protest my first love was West Ham, based on my time growing up in London. The driver suggested that my support for the Villa was superficially based purely on the colour of their cherished strip. I was mildly abashed by this suggestion. After being dropped off around mid-morning by the local post office in Cutnall Green, I went inside to buy some water and chocolate, wherein the serving lady enquired enthusiastically after my purpose. I explained my mission, to which she generously responded in a positive manner, offering me directions. I strolled back past the previously visited pub to pick up the lane to Elmley Lovett.

A MIDLAND MEANDER

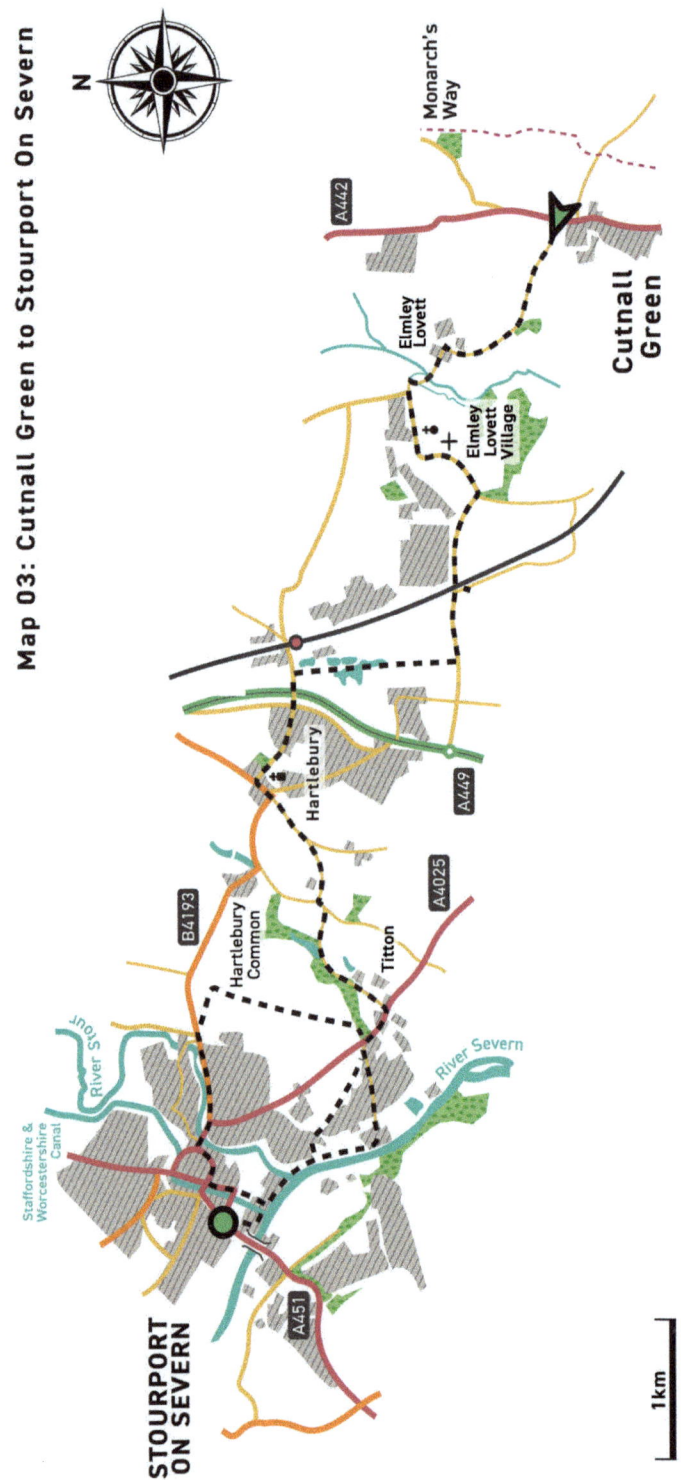

I trekked up to the hamlet of Elmley Lovett, comprised of Upton Farm and the grand house and a couple of other nice dwellings, evidence of a medieval origin. I plodded on down to the significant stream which is the Hockley Brook, originating in the south-western edge of the Midland plateau and flowing through Chaddesley Corbett and down to the River Salwarpe, south-west of Droitwich. I carried on past the church and observed lumps and bumps in a field, thankfully not ploughed, the site of a lost medieval village. At a field corner at sixty-five metres, I leant on a gate observing the scene northwards. I could clearly see the Paps of Clent. This is an allusion to the Paps of Jura in the Hebrides, two adjacent and identical twin hills with a pronounced valley in-between. Given that I have always been fond of Paps, it has greatly amused me to draw this comparison, even though the cleavage is less pronounced than the Scottish example. Continuing on, I elected to take the laborious lane past the incongruous trading estate and under the railway, not the most pleasant stretch of this traverse across North Worcestershire. I passed under the railway and progressed onto another ordnance survey map; from Landranger 139 to Landranger 138. After the railway line I chose to take a well-marked footpath, northwards towards Hartlebury.

I came across a group of mature pear trees dripping with fruit, remnants perhaps of an old orchard, and I wondered whether they could be of the black Worcester variety, now distinctly rare, famed in heraldry. The coat of arms of the city of Worcester and the badge of Worcestershire County cricket club all exhibit these black pears. I passed through metal kissing gates protecting small horse paddocks. Then I stumbled across a collection of large fishing lakes, one of which was hosting a deadly serious fishing match. Speaking to one chap getting ready to fish, he informed me that the lakes contained all types of freshwater fish except the predatory pike whose Latin name, *Esox lucius*, alludes to it being named as the devil fish and not welcome in a carefully overstocked lake. These were well-appointed fishing grounds with their own café and toilet facilities, a testament to one of our most popular outdoor pastimes. I came up to the top lane and turned west, passing under the A449 dual carriageway, effectively forming the Hartlebury bypass.

Dog-legging through a subsidiary centre to the main village, with a redundant pub and a general store, I trudged down the steep hill to the village centre, with a curious mixture of old cottages and newer houses squeezed in-between, perching at rakish angles on the slope. In the centre of the village, I stood outside the striking red sandstone church, no doubt built in the Triassic bedrock. Crossing over the road, I intended to sample the beer on offer in The White Hart Hotel. I sat in the gloomy public front bar and consumed a single pint of beer, while listening to the grumbles of other customers who discovered that the food was off that day. I quite fancied a sandwich, or something like that, but it was not to be.

Leaving the pub, after what was, to be frank, an underwhelming experience, I took the small lane opposite the pub towards Hartlebury Common. Strolling down through a damp, wooded valley containing the Hillditch Pool, a Site of Special Scientific Interest, on the southern edge of the common, I came up to the A4025 in the vicinity of Titton. I turned right along the main road, towards Stourport, for a short distance, before locating Sandy Lane. Opposite this turning, the common opened up, showing itself as sparse, sandy lowland heath of 229 acres, a distinctly rare habitat, forming a river terrace of the Severn with windblown sand overlying the sandstone beds of the Triassic geological period. At the corner of Sandy Lane, the much-anticipated pub had been converted to an Indian restaurant, looking

Hartlebury Church © Philip Halling

distinctly shabby. I plodded on towards the river through an active, disorganised industrial estate before disgorging into a massive, regimented riverside holiday caravan park.

I emerged triumphantly on the bank of the mighty River Severn and strolled northwards towards Stourport. After about half a mile, I crossed over the River Stour, flowing back through Kidderminster and Stourbridge, joining at the Severn at this point, by an elegant brick-built humpbacked bridge. I saw a baby wren marooned on the bridge, trying to hide in the brick crevices. I was tempted to pick the bird up and move it somewhere else because I couldn't see it surviving in such an exposed position, but I thought better of it because it was well camouflaged against the brick parapet, and I concluded that its parents new best. After this crossing, I strolled on past a waterfront of imposing dilapidated industrial buildings, with huge development potential. Then I reached The Angel Inn, a splendidly located elegant riverside pub. I sat outside and enjoyed ham sandwiches and several pints of real ale, basking in warm autumn sunshine.

The Angel Inn, Stourport © Roger Kidd

Just past the pub, I reached the spot where the Staffordshire and Worcestershire Canal, designed and built by James Brindley, joined the River Severn. Here was an amazingly well-manicured complex of locks and canal basins, given over entirely to leisure pursuits connected with boating. However, formerly this was a massively busy inland port where the manufactured goods from Birmingham and the West Midlands and the Potteries, and the raw materials to support those industries, were transhipped. To my right, up a gentle slope, was the solidly impressive building of the Tontine Hotel. This building was completed in 1772 and formed the headquarters of the Staffordshire and Worcestershire Canal company. I recalled on a previous walk up the Severn Way to Ironbridge, I had stayed in another hotel, directly opposite the iconic Iron Bridge, also thus called. The word 'tontine' is derived from an Italian, Lorenzo Tonti, who devised an early form of life insurance. In this scheme, members paid into a fund which accrued over the years and was paid out to the last surviving member. It did cross my mind whether the promised bounty at the end of the arrangement would encourage some members to bump off their competitors. I imagine many hotels across the country were named

The Tontine, Stourport © Philip Pankhurst

after this activity, presumably because meetings of the group were held there. I wondered if there are any such examples of this practice in Italy.

I walked on through the complex, past some lovely old canalside cottages towards Stourport high street. I stood for a while on a humpbacked bridge of elegant proportions and admired a narrowboat deftly manoeuvring itself through locks steeply descending to the big river. Caroline Hillier, in her book *A Journey to the Heart of England* published in 1976, eloquently described the scene as follows:

> *So round the basin at Stourport were built the fine canal buildings: Georgian red-brick terrace cottages and wharfs, The Tontine Inn which was originally five houses used by hop merchants, and a red-brick warehouse with a white cupola, which is now the Stourport Yacht Club. It is uncluttered as if still in the canal era, a superb arrangement of low buildings and white lock woodwork, surrounded by a maze of locks, then streets of Georgian houses spreading from the town centre, with the rush of the Severn water below the sloping lawns of the Tontine.*

Forty-three years later, I felt that this description still accurately described the scene in Stourport, although the Tontine hotel had now been converted into residential properties. I noted that this book would feature many of the places that I intended to visit on my own perambulation around the West Midlands conurbation, the only difference being that I was walking, and she wasn't always.

Having passed the yacht club, by another large inland basin bedecked by a multitude of colourful canal boats, I hit the bottom of the high street, just up from the Severn bridge. I strolled up the busy street and popped into The Wheatsheaf, a historic pub in the middle of the high street. While supping my pint in a badly lit corner of the front bar, I tried to avoid the attentions of a small, yappy resident dog who seemed to want to make friends and sit on my lap. I felt the pub had that same run-down air that I had remarked on before, about the pubs in Bromsgrove high street. While waiting outside for a local bus to take me to Kidderminster, raising my gaze above the busy shop frontages, I observed the regular rhythm of the Georgian buildings in the high street referred to by Hillier. Eccentrically, this has been my habit in many different towns over the years, waiting outside particularly boring shops, selling useless novelty items, waiting for a female companion to emerge from within.

Stourport-on-Severn

> River and canal
> Lost enterprise
> Georgian splendour
> A quaint surprise
> East bank of the mighty stream.

Boarding the bus, I enquired of the driver the best way to get back home, but he could offer no better advice than to go to Kidderminster, so I went there. In the functional bus station in the form of a gigantic oval, I enquired of an elderly couple minding their own business, crouched timidly in a shelter, of the best bus to catch to get me back to Birmingham. I got the impression that the big metropolis was outside their normal patch, but they did suggest there was no direct route and that I would have to go via Halesowen. Searching for a bus shelter sign to that effect, I saw a bus destined for Bromsgrove, so I changed plan, chased it and jumped on board, since I knew a taxi would be waiting in Bromsgrove to ferry me back to the big city. The bus trundled rather quickly along the twisty A448, through the undulating North Worcestershire countryside, through Mustow Green and past Chaddesley Corbett to Bromsgrove, where, as anticipated, a taxi was there ready to whisk me back to Birmingham.

Returning to Stourport after a few weeks, in mid-October I checked into the very same Angel Inn. This was the first time on this trek around the West Midlands conurbation that I had booked accommodation, since up to this point, I was able conveniently to pop back home. I wanted to stay in this promising riverside pub and also, as a slight diversion, have a good look around Hartlebury Common. I parked my car at the pub, changed into walking boots and strode out past canal basins, one of which had been developed for up-market residential apartments. I always wonder in apparently up-market, watery situations like this, in canal-side developments, whether the inevitable prevalence of rats would take the edge off the experience.

Passing through the outskirts of the town, I crossed over the River Stour and picked up the B4193, the Hartlebury Road, which took me up onto the common, designated as an SSSI in 1955. I climbed up to the bare, damaged, pockmarked top, a high point of fifty-six metres, and headed due south. I observed a profusion of gorse, heather and broom growing on the intensely sandy soil of this lowland heath. In the centre of the common I passed a number of ancient oak trees dwarfed by the impoverished soil and their exposed position. Scrambling down off the common, I careered along a soft, sandy track with my boots sinking deep into the sand. I thought this sand could easily be bagged up for building sand as no doubt it would have been in the past, before the common was protected. Coming down off the high common, there were lovely views of what appeared to be the slightly less austere lower common straddling the main A4025.

On reaching the main road, at the same point where I passed

Stunted oak tree, Hartlebury Common

Hartlebury Common © Richard Greenwood

through a few weeks before, I popped into the local Titton stores for water and chocolate. I asked directions from the obliging Asian owner about the best route back to Stourport. He suggested I walk across the lower common and back to the big river. This was, however, a quite disappointing section of this circular walk in that the path hugged the ragged back of the industrial estate in Sandy Lane which I had previously tackled and the common here was churned up by the unbridled use of four-wheeled vehicles, driven, I imagine, as a noisy leisure pursuit by local lads. I plodded on along badly rutted paths under electricity pylons while being aggressively challenged by local dogs out for their morning exercise. Certainly, the lower common looked more appealing from a distance, from the vantage point back on the high common.

Coming back to the river through a new ubiquitous housing estate on the outskirts of Stourport, I retraced my steps up to the Stour bridge. I noted again the derelict buildings hard up against the river, and, as I was to find out later, they were the site of a famous vinegar factory which was brewing this condiment here, starting in 1798, until its closure in 2000. I thought vinegar was made from wood, but it transpires that vinegar can be brewed from virtually anything. I returned to The Angel Inn, booked in and made the acquaintance of the landlord. In the evening, I went for a stroll around the town in the gathering gloom, but mostly spent a very pleasant time in the pub. I watched an England football match against Bulgaria in a World Cup qualifying match, which England won 5-0. This match was marred by the appalling racist chants emanating from a small local group of Nazi-sympathising thugs.

In the morning I made my way back to Bridge Street to find a café for a full English breakfast, as the pub was not able to oblige. Then, suitably fed, I dropped down through a car park adjacent to a dormant funfair and dived under the main road by a generously arched brick tunnel. I strode out along the riverside, past a large park flanked by oak trees, home to a scurry of squirrels, fruitlessly chased by local dogs let off their leads for a run around. I strolled on beside the powerful brown river, effortlessly sweeping large lumps of debris downstream. The banks of the river were lined with pleasure boats, carefully moored on private stations, with charging points behind forbidding metal fences. These premises belonged to the Stourport Motor Yacht & Bungalow Association, providing lots of static holiday homes for weekenders from the Midlands. This occurrence of holiday homes and caravans by inland rivers is a feature which is seemingly unique to the Midlands, probably because the coast is a long way away. I mused on the fact that the last time I tackled this stretch of the Severn Way was in 2004, and having trekked from Worcester and aiming for Bewdley that day, a mere twenty-four miles, I was so knackered – head down, intent on covering the ground – that I failed to record any details of this part of the journey. On that occasion, I was headed eventually for Shrewsbury, calling in at Bridgenorth and Ironbridge on the way, a riverine trek, northwards along the Severn Way.

I noticed along this stretch of the river that the banks were almost always privately owned and used for various leisure activities including long reaches occupied by fishing associations. After a wet early October, this uneven path was treacherous and as I slithered gingerly along, I noticed the banks were clothed mainly with willow, invasive Himalayan balsam and blue-flowered borage. I reached a point where I had to detour away from the river around a compound where works

A MIDLAND MEANDER

Map 04: Stourport On Severn to Bewdley

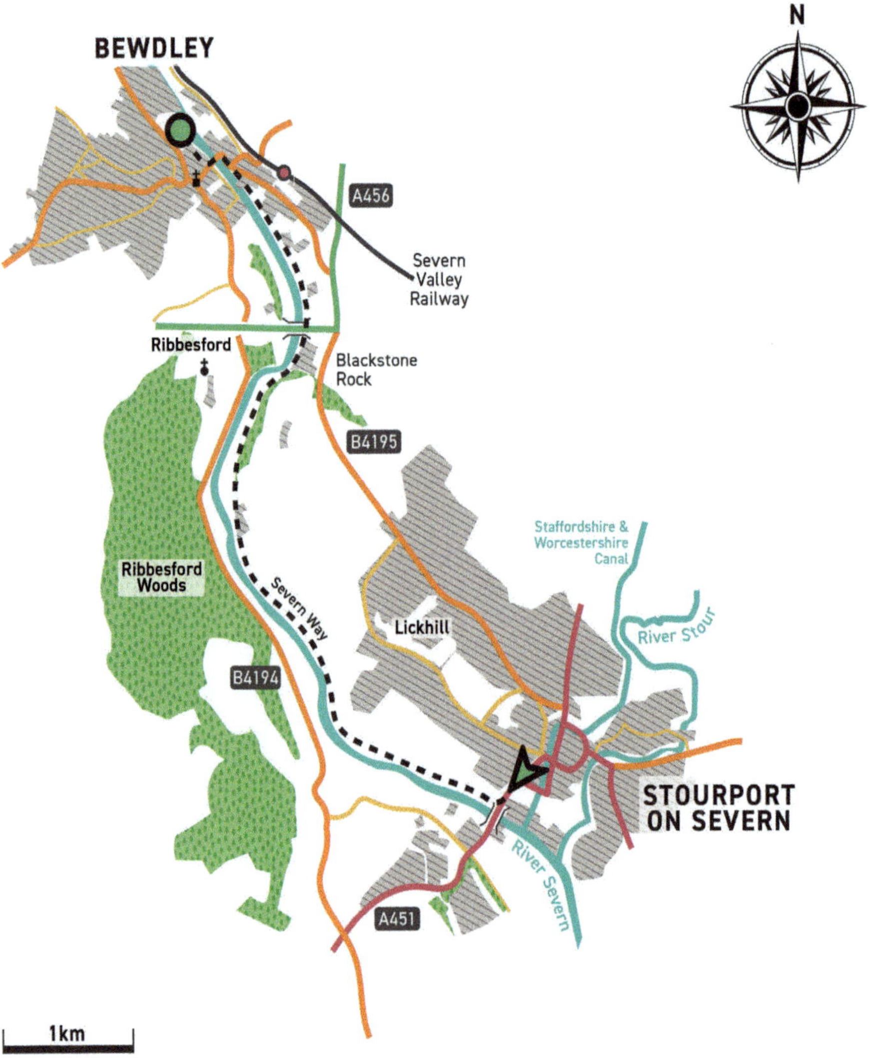

were in progress to lay a twenty-six-kilometre pipeline from this point at Lickhills to supply water from the river to Birmingham, effectively supplementing the supply provided by the Elan Valley scheme, relieving mid-Wales of excessive water. After this temporary scar on the landscape, I reached Severn Bank Park which exhibited some rather splendid static homes, raised up on a bank, overlooking the river. Further on, in an area designated as a country park, I hit a dramatic new red sandstone river cliff known as Blackstone rock. I stood for a while and admired the robust strata towering above me. The Severn Way at this point passes through a sandstone rock gorge before returning to the riverbank. Pressing on, I passed underneath the A456 road bridge which effectively bypasses the pleasant riverside town of Bewdley.

I came into Bewdley along the eastern bank, all the while admiring the townscape on the western quayside across the impressively wide and immensely powerful river. In the past, this bank would have been lined with boats and barges when Bewdley was an important inland port in the seventeenth century, and many of the fashionable residential

The River Severn at Bewdley © Matt Fascione

buildings on the quayside would have been warehouses and commercial offices. I crossed over the elegant bridge built by Thomas Telford in 1798, now carrying sufficient traffic to consign pedestrians to a very narrow footpath squeezed up against the parapet. I thought public investment in a separate pedestrian bridge would have considerable merit, and, if well designed, should enhance the appeal of the town. After a quick stroll up the elegant main street, known as The Load, I searched for a bus to take me back to Stourport, where my car was located.

I enquired after a bus and was told by friendly locals to cross over the road. Immediately after skipping across The Load, the bus pulled up and I opportunistically jumped on and was transported back to Stourport. Approaching the town, I passed through the substantial, if somewhat mundane, suburb called Lickhills, in the vicinity of the waterworks previously passed down by the river. Disembarking in the Stourport high street, I retraced my steps around the canal basins, along the warmly bricked passage, named Engine Lane, back to The Angel Inn. I drove back to Bewdley along the same route and checked into the popular Mug House Inn on the west bank, after negotiating complex parking arrangements in the Dog Lane car park.

After a pleasant interlude, eating and drinking in the pub, and the statutory rest, I explored the town. From the high street, running parallel with the river, I strolled down past St Anne's church along the noticeably wide Lode Street, which used to hold a market, down to the quayside. Load is an old Shropshire name for a ferry, as epitomised by the name of the Severnside village of Hampton Loade further up the river, and the main street in Bewdley would have accessed a similar crossing before the bridge was built. I reflected on the fact that here in Bewdley I was at the most western point of my perambulation around the West Midlands conurbation. Strolling along the quayside, admiring the fast-flowing river, I observed the locking positions set in the ground from which robust flood defences could be speedily erected when required. Later on, in this winter, in February 2020, these defences were severely tested. I am glad to say that they successfully held out, much to the relief of the residents and businesses on the west bank; unfortunately, the east bank, where I came into the town, didn't fare so well and were completely inundated. I had a pleasant meal in the restaurant attached to the inn and whiled away the rest of the evening in the pub. In the morning after breakfast, I returned home to Kings Heath in South Birmingham to plan the next leg of my journey.

A few weeks later, I returned to Bewdley to continue my trek northwards through Worcestershire. From the Dog Lane car park, I struck out along the quayside. I chanced upon a flock of seven geese nonchalantly disported on the quayside, seemingly unphased by passing foot traffic. These were the native Greylag geese from which all domestic geese were bred, making themselves perfectly at home on this Severn shore. Crossing back over Telford's impressive bridge, I passed out of Bewdley under the railway. There were some obviously old buildings on the east bank in the vicinity of Beale's corner, not faring very well in this busy approach to the town. This included The Black Boy Inn, a hostelry that I had stayed in many years ago on my previous ramble up the Severn Valley, in a run-down area on the eastern bank, not helped by the propensity of the big river to seriously and repeatedly flood here.

Bewdley

Seven geese on Severn shore

> *Severnside town*
> *Elegant quay*
> *Geese holding sway*
> *Flooding free*
> *Due to massive riverside defences*

Peeling off to the left through housing estates of a district called Wribbenhall, rising all the time, I traipsed along Grey Green Lane. As I climbed up to a farm complex, the lowering mist covering the higher ground enveloped me. I took a footpath across damp fields to join the lane to Trimpley at a height of ninety-eight metres. At this point, while trying to gain access to the lane, endeavouring to cross a soggy ditch, I sank into the mud which covered my boots. Reaching the desired lane by scrambling through a thicket, I attempted to clean off the excessive mud by rubbing my boots through long grass. Pressing on towards Trimpley, past Wassell Wood, managed by the Woodlands Trust, with its integral earthwork, I climbed up to an elevation of 176 metres. The lane was uncomfortable walking with speeding traffic much in evidence, and the lowering mist was depressing.

I took a short detour into the centre of Trimpley village just to see what was there. There wasn't much there except a church and village hall and a few houses, so I cut across fields behind the church to regain the lane northwards. I carried on climbing up to a height of 202 metres before descending into the hamlet of Shatterford, where the fitful sun eventually broke through. There were some pleasant dwellings in the hamlet before the busy main A442 Bridgenorth Road. I popped into The Bellmans Cross Inn for lunch. This ancient inn was geared up for diners, and I felt a little awkward propping up the bar eating my croque monsieur. The copious lashings of salad made the offering more a meal than a snack. I did, however, make the harassed barmaid laugh when ordering, describing this pretentiously named French snack as posh cheese and ham on toast. After a few pints, I got the barmaid to order me a taxi back to Bewdley, which dropped me off at The Black Boy Inn.

ALVECHURCH TO KINVER

Map 05: Bewdley to Kinver

Before ambling back to my car over the river, I had occasion to pop into the pub again out of curiosity. The premises, a listed building, seemed much reduced from when I stayed a night in the summer of 2004. I engaged the barmaid there in conversation regarding the pub's name. She explained that it was a meeting place for followers of Charles II during the English Civil War, the pub's name being an ironic toast that was raised to Charles II due to his dusky hue. I imagined cavaliers in their finery sitting there, managing the kings flight after defeat at the battle of Worcester. After a single pint and a decent rest in the Dog Lane car park, I drove back to Birmingham.

Returning a few weeks later, I was domiciled in The Fox Inn at Stourton on the Bridgenorth Road. I spent a pleasant evening in the pub propping up the bar, chatting to locals and the bar staff in this very popular pub. I made the acquaintance of the energetic Welsh landlord who proudly pointed out to me a plaque behind the bar announcing the winning of the *Four in a Bed* television programme. The locals were concerned that the pub would become even more popular as a result of winning this competition. I had a large, well-appointed room in the roof space which thankfully was delightfully warm and comfortable, so I'm not surprised the pub won this prestigious competition.

In the bright new morning, I caught a taxi back to Bellmans Cross, thinking that Bellman, whoever he was, would not be that annoyed. The shy Asian driver from Stourbridge seemed most uncomfortable and out of his comfort zone in the foreign countryside. I had to direct him through country lanes with the aid of my map, a concept which he seemed to have difficulty in grasping. My failure to provide a postcode that he could punch into his dashboard machine seemed to faze him greatly. Disembarking outside The Bellmans Cross Inn, previously visited, I strode off down the lane back to Shatterford. At the top of the hamlet, I located the Worcestershire Way and got into my stride. After a short stretch I came back to the main A442 which I crossed with care. I picked up a footpath and trundled off the hillside affording spectacular views northwards over the Worcestershire and South Staffordshire countryside. The superb landscape in these parts is a mix of pasture, woodland and arable land. A few miles north from here is the place where three counties meet: the above mentioned and Shropshire. I could clearly see Kinver Edge in the distance where I was headed. Sauntering on beside a fledgling stream floating long grass to the surface, I passed some ancient ash trees with fantastically contorted trunks.

I plunged down the steep slope to the lane below, through a field with three large friendly horses who approached me for a stroke. I always feel that it would be churlish to refuse these equine advances

Stunted ash tree, Worcestershire Way

even though I have no experience of horses. Having been lulled into a false sense of security by the well-marked footpath so far, I have to confess that I did lose my intended way here. There was no sign indicating the route through a static caravan park, which I guess had been deliberately removed, and I ended up plodding up the lane in the wrong direction. I soon smelt a rat and reorientated myself with the aid of my mobile phone. This is the first time I have used this device in this way, since the map application has the distinct advantage of letting one know exactly where one is and in what direction one is facing. At a sharp bend in the lane, which was going nowhere, I took a footpath, past a paddock with a host of charming goats, and worked my way back to the other side of the caravan park, about a half mile detour. Reorientated, I shuffled along beside a bubbling stream that flows down to the River Stour in Kidderminster.

Then I slogged up a curving road past many more static-caravan-type homes to Blakeshall Common. The communities of Drakelow and Kingsford in this vicinity, in the very north-western edge of Worcestershire, close to the county boundary, appear to almost entirely consist of hundreds of these prefabricated dwellings. It is almost as though this somewhat unconventional settlement pattern could only be tolerated by the planning authorities at the northern most extremities of the county, where seemingly it didn't matter too much. On this stretch I passed the entrance to the Drakelow tunnels, a shadow factory set up in the Second World War, as a safe place to relocate vital manufacturing activities from Birmingham. They consist of three and a half miles of tunnels dug into the soft sandstone rock beneath Kingsford Country Park, which are now under the care of a Preservation Trust set up by locals to thwart the development of the site for a more useful and a no doubt more invasive purpose. Having said that, I can't see these tunnels being a major tourist attraction: so, what to do with them? I guess they could be used for growing mushrooms!

In crossing Blakeshall Common, I picked up the Worcestershire Way again, passing through swathes of pine trees thriving on the red soil. The tall sentinel trees seemed almost as red as the soil. Further on, I asked a couple out walking their dog what was the best way to get to Kinver Edge. They advised me to turn round and take the eastern track up the hill. After a stiff climb up to Kingsford Country Park festooned with groups of elderly ramblers with a multitude of sticks, many of whom I guess were no older than me, I pressed on towards the high sandstone ridge. I reached the point where three long-distance paths meet; namely the Worcestershire Way, the North Worcestershire Path and the Staffordshire Way and, taking the latter, passed on, expectantly, into South Staffordshire.

Up on the Edge there were stunning views off the steep escarpment across the undulating terrain to the west, towards Alveley and the River Severn. At intervals along the Edge, the trees cloaking the precipitous slope had been cut down to open up the panorama viewed from carefully located benches in an area managed by the National Trust. On one bench there was an assemblage of floral tributes, no doubt commemorating the ending of a life at the steepest point of the escarpment. I observed a herd of long-horn cattle lazily grazing the hillside, whose purpose, in this case, was to keep at bay the invasive Himalayan balsam. This attractive, fast-growing, greedy annual weed, if left to itself, spreads mercilessly by active seed dispersal and shades out our native flora, gradually impoverishing the soil.

Further on, still climbing, I reached a trig point at 164 metres. From here there were fabulous views out eastwards towards Stourbridge and the Black Country. This was my patch when I worked in the planning department of Dudley Borough Council for a couple of years in the mid-'70s. The second slightly higher trig point at 166 metres was the culmination of the Edge before the Staffordshire Way plunged down into Kinver. I would have studied the compass map showing directed views from the stone turret construction located at the highest point, the same edifice I have seen on my own Lickey Hills, but it was surrounded by an impenetrable gaggle of tourists savouring this local beauty spot. Instead, I paused for a while in a quiet corner and gazed northwards over the South Staffordshire countryside envisaging my future perambulation.

Descending from the Edge by a steep path, I came to the famous rock houses, which now seem to be of sufficient interest to warrant National Trust care. These troglodyte dwellings were occupied until the 1960s and are carved out of the soft Triassic dune sand rock, laid down in desert conditions. I remembered years ago visiting these dilapidated caves without having to pay an entrance fee. Today, the caves are greatly sanitised and coming in by the back door off the Edge, I was challenged by a lady gatekeeper when leaving by the legitimate entrance. After explaining my progress, and stating that I was only trying to follow the footpath, she reluctantly relented and allowed me not to pay an exit fee. I sidled down the unstable hillside to the next lane, which doubled up as a car park for the cave facilities, and worked my way down to Potter Cross, missing out on the reputedly unremarkable centre of Kinver.

I climbed up the rise through suburban houses on the long, straight road to Enville and branched off right to reach my destination, The Fox Inn on the A458. I spent another very pleasant evening in the pub, eating and drinking, and talking to locals at the bar. I complimented the Welsh landlord, who was evidently older than me, on his splendid pub, and he generously rewarded me with a free pint. I was introduced to an elderly fellow rambler who recounted his experiences of trekking in the Lake District, paying tribute to Alfred Wainright, that doyen

Holy Austin rock houses near Kinver in Staffordshire © Roger Kidd

of our walking tribe. I always feel slightly in awe of fellow walkers who have tackled areas in the north of the country, such as the Lake District, and hope they don't underestimate my efforts in South East England and now in the West Midlands.

In the morning after breakfast, I returned home relatively satisfied, having taken advantage of a couple of dry days in late October in a very wet autumn. I drove back through the centre of Kinver and revised my opinion of the place. Contrary to what I was told in the pub, it seemed a perfectly pleasant large village nestling under its impressive Edge. I reckoned I had completed nearly a quarter of my planned journey around the conurbation; the remaining three quarters would now have to wait until the next year and better weather.

Chapter Two

Kinver to Brewood

When the better weather arrived in late March, my intended resumption of the circumnavigation of the West Midlands conurbation in the spring of 2020 was brutally curtailed by the disastrous global coronavirus pandemic. Sitting at home, self-isolating, trapped in my study, I started to read again books that I first read as a teenager, many decades ago. In particular, I enjoyed once again the novels relating to tramps: Herman Hesse's *Knulp* and *The Autobiography of a Super-Tramp* by W. H. Davies. I realised then that my predilection to go rambling was my own pathetic attempt to experience the freedom of the open road and to achieve that sense of being an outsider looking in, which both of the above books vividly illustrate. A situation that gives a brief respite from the multifarious demands on one's time in a normal existence and as a form of escapism. In this way, I could enjoy the hospitality offered by various hotels and pubs on the route for a while before passing on to the next stop, where new and novel experiences always beckon. However, the life of a tramp is ultimately self-destructive and must come to a whimpering end, as both of the above examples demonstrate. I hope to avoid this outcome for as long as possible before being forced to hang up my boots for the final time, as long as the dreadful virus doesn't get me first.

As our enforced inactivity dragged on through the summer of 2020, I resurrected a trio of lugubrious, if portentous, poems, I wrote a few years before as follows: '*A Rock to Call Our Own*', '*The Fragility of Life*' and '*Ash Cloud*'. I offer them here as an antidote to the debilitating effects of Covid-19. I feel my pessimism exhibited in this trio of poems in a way predicted the appalling effects of the virus and reflects how fragile our present way of life is.

A Rock to Call Our Own
As I staggered home from the pub
Bowed by the burden of the beer
Turning the corner of the street
Trying to stay upon my feet
I saw spring catkins strewn around
Emerald carpet on the ground
And, wallowing in that parlous state,
I had a vision of our fate.

Imagining this verdant sward
Carried away by countless rains
Run off down inefficient drains
Combined with our toxic waste
Festering slowly in the depths
The very noxious effluent
Of our tenuous existence
The sludge of civilisation.

Eventually, many aeons hence,
Flushed down polluted waterways
Sedimentary under seas
Compressed and compacted, thence,
In distinctive multicoloured strata
Left with a plastic signature
A new geological period
We might have a rock to call our own.

Wondering if Homo sapiens
Would still be flourishing, extant,
Or whether some other species
Would be concerned to dig it up
Examine it curiously
As morbid archaeology
Much as we are fascinated
By the plight of the dinosaurs.

Fragility of Life
As I become older
Closer to my demise
I am concerned about
The fragility of life
In a sort of distracted
Voyeuristic sort of way.

A bug-virulent outbreak
Another meteorite strike
Or simply an imbalance
In our atmospheric chemistry
Could easily cause our
Civilisation to collapse.

Then all our marvellous
Achievements and
Scientific advances
Attempts to control
Our volatile world
Will come to nothing.

Understanding all this
Knowing that our sun
Will eventually die

Accepting the human
Species is transient
And will disappear.

Given this knowledge
This entropic reality
Why should I take
Life so seriously?

Ash Cloud
An ash cloud
High up in the sky
From a volcano
In Iceland
Destroys our ability
To fly planes safely
Shakes our world
To its core.

Imagine what
It would have been like
For the dinosaurs
When their world
Was thrown into darkness
By debris put up
Into the atmosphere
By a meteorite hitting the earth
And a supervolcano
Erupting simultaneously
In India creating
The Deccan traps.

Devastating!
Covering the globe

> In a dense black cloud
> Blocking out the sun
> Destroying vegetation
> Starving animals
> To death in a few years
> So that only insipient
> Ground-burrowing
> Mammals could survive
> Creatures that have evolved
> Over elongated time into us.

I'm pleased to say that the virus – that tragically killed so many people – even though I was in the so-called vulnerable group, didn't get me, and I was able to resume my ambitious journey in late July, wondering whether life would ever be the same again. I made my next base in The Red Lion in Bobbington, a small village in South Staffordshire close to the border with Shropshire. Even after many months, since Covid-19 took hold on our lives, the experience was a very strange and different one which required a degree of adaptability on my part to make it work. I reasoned, with the virus having abated somewhat, with the judicious wearing of face masks, I could travel through the countryside relatively safely.

I arrived at The Red Lion Bobbington, after driving through the Black Country via Stourbridge, with its racetrack ring road, on a dismal, rain-soaked day, not fit for walking. I gained entry to my venue and found a key with a note on the deserted reception desk, so I settled into my adequate room. After a short rest, and the rain having cleared, I decided to have a look round the village. There was a long, curving street inhabited by perfectly comfortable but mundane dwellings, commuter land for Wolverhampton and Bridgenorth. A traditional church was prefaced by a very untidy swathe of land which I guess would be full of parked cars in more populous worshiping times. I strolled out to the back of the ample pub car park and observed a most altogether-more-appealing view of the church across a gulley with sheep-nibbled fields. In all honesty though, Bobbington

The Red Lion Inn at Bobbington © Roger Kidd

is a most unremarkable village. After a splendid meal, I sat out the evening in the pub and made the acquaintance of brothers running the pub and the regular barmaids.

After a short taxi ride, I started my perambulation again from the lane below the Rock Houses in Kinver and strode out westwards to pick up the Staffordshire Way. At the top of the short rise, I picked up a small lane going northwards towards White Hill farm, where I joined the long-distance footpath. It was a good, bright, sunny morning although cool for late July; ideal walking weather to appreciate the spectacular views across the South Staffordshire countryside and back to Kinver Edge. After a brief descent to a small stream, I climbed up through a narrow sandstone gorge eroded by countless feet and hooves on this bridleway over the years. This is strong new red sandstone country laid down in the Triassic geological period many trillions of years ago. The gently undulating path led me all the way to the grounds of Enville Hall, a well-kept estate with neat paddocks full of horses.

KINVER TO BREWOOD

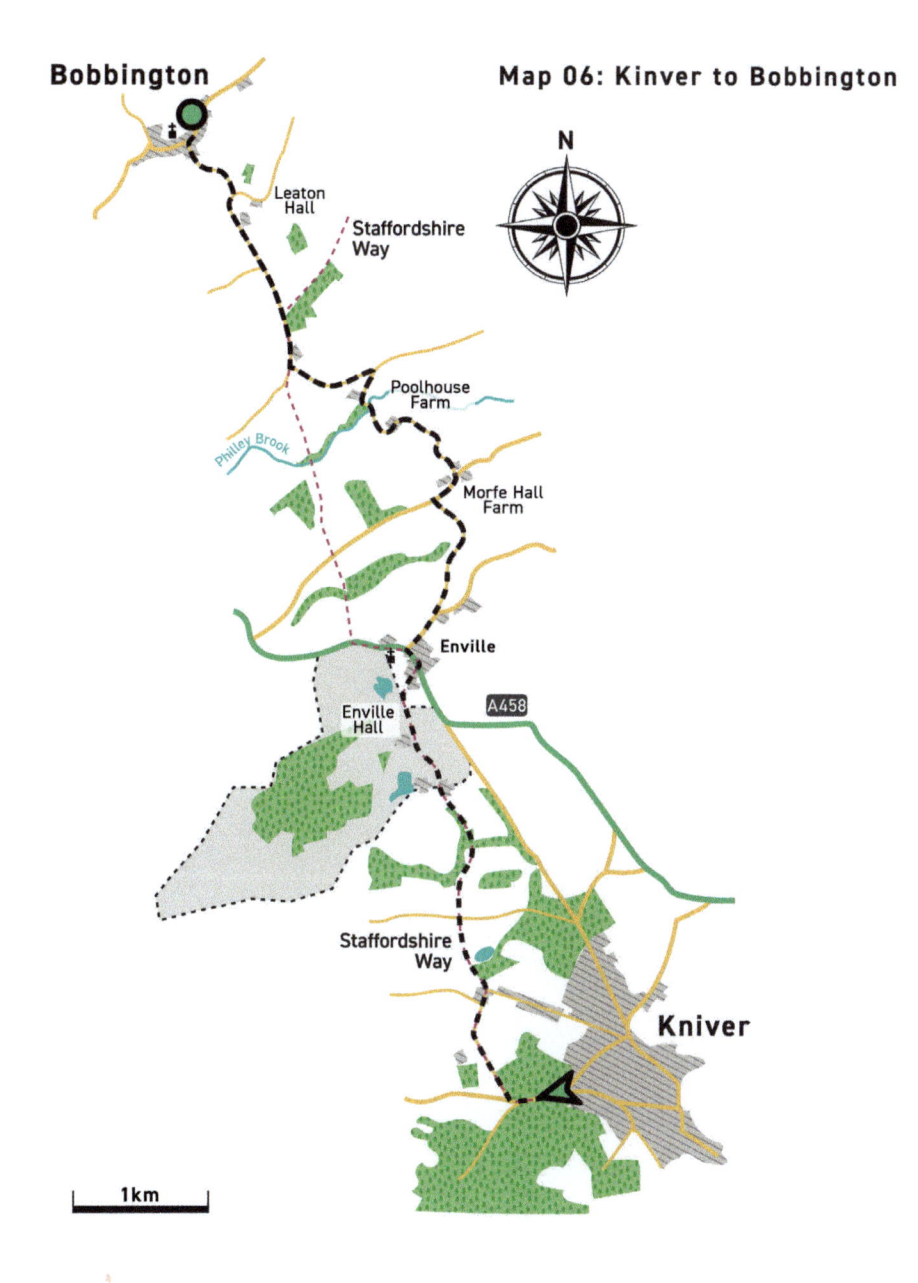

Map 06: Kinver to Bobbington

Reaching the hall, I stood still for a while outside the main entrance, which appeared to be through a delightful timeless stable block fronting the drive. I observed the inhabitants milling about inside and imagined one of the party driving off carelessly, throwing up the gravel in a Range Rover. Really, I wanted to go inside and explore this extravagant, if somewhat appealing, foreign, and probably not sustainable, lifestyle. Opposite was a sumptuous, well-presented cricket ground with house martins gracing the scene. Even the scoreboard, housed in a quaint hut against the stable block wall, enhanced the prospect, but was mainly, I guess, only appreciated by cricket lovers like me. The prospect lit an indulgent reverie of long years of partaking in our wonderful summer game.

Researching Enville Cricket Club, I was to find that it was very old, founded in 1821 with a long history, supported by the lord of the manor. More recently, the club plays in the Worcestershire league, although it is firmly in Staffordshire, on an impressive, well-constructed ground. I imagined this would be a good, flat batting wicket, where it would be possible, with some technique, to build an innings, a privilege that mostly I have had denied to me through thirty years of playing the game, often on park pitches. I recalled a match on the old Worcestershire County ground at Dudley, when I worked for the local authority there, with sections of the outfield fenced off to guard against sink holes caused by past coal mining activities. On this good wicket, definitely not a park pitch, formerly used by professional players, I was able to stroke the ball around and build up a good score. I guess I felt that this reminiscence reminded me of my youth and my old stamping ground in Kent where I struggled to play well on many dodgy wickets. A little further on

Scoreboard at Enville Cricket Club
© John M

I observed what appeared to be a large, disused walled garden, and I indulged in another fantasy. Although I couldn't be sure that the walled garden was in fact derelict, I thought it would be a wonderful project to bring it back into productive use. Coming into Enville, along a long, curving drive, beside a high wall, there were some pretty cottages at the main entrance to the estate on the Bridgenorth Road.

I reached The Cat public house at ten-thirty, too early for a drink, even if that was possible in these Covid-19 times. The pub was only open for pre-booked tables and not available to me as a passing stranger, which in my mind defeats the primary purpose of a pub. However, in these Covid-19-ravaged times, I guess it was a sensible precaution. When I had stayed up the road last year, in The Fox Inn, it had been recommended to me as a place where there was good beer. I resigned myself to the acceptance that this pub would escape my perusal this time around. The village has some attractive antique cottages with an imposing red church perched on the nearby hill, largely spoilt, unfortunately, by the thunderous traffic on the narrow and twisty A458. My natural instinct in situations like this, being a qualified town planner, is to search for a route of a bypass to relieve the village of through traffic. Because of the curve of the A458 through Enville, the shortest obverse angle route would be the south, but this would sever the village from the Enville Hall estate; not a satisfactory outcome. The wider reflex angle and more expensive, longer route would be to the north of the village, making it difficult to justify. Thus, I concluded that Enville would have to put up with the through traffic for the foreseeable future.

Departing from the Staffordshire Way, I struck out down quiet lanes towards Morfe Hall Farm. Looking at the map, I noticed many halls in the vicinity, less grand no doubt than Enville, but nevertheless forming rather splendid houses. I noted there were many characterful red-brick barns ripe for conversion to desirable dwellings in a lovely rural location. I felt that it would be a shame to lose these attractive buildings to dereliction if they had no useful agricultural purpose. Looking back southwards, where I had come from, I could clearly see Kinver Edge picked out on the skyline. I reached the Philley Brook

The A458 at Enville © P. L. Chadwick

and leant on the bridge parapet for a while, observing the deeply cut stream choked by dull red sediment washed out of the surrounding landscape.

As I trekked ever northwards, I was traversing the Mid Severn sandstone plateau laid down in the Triassic and Permian geological periods. The slight undulations in the terrain were created by a number of insipient streams eating into the bedrock running south-west down to the Severn via the rivers Worfe and Stour or northwards via the River Penk to the Trent, effectively forming a major watershed between two major English rivers, the Severn and Trent. This West Midlands National Character Area 66, defined by Natural England, was a delight, graced as it is by rich agricultural land with red soil and a generous scattering of estate parklands. The River Severn cuts through this plateau to the west which stretches from Kidderminster in the south to Telford in the north, straddling the South Staffordshire/Shropshire county border.

After the Philley Brook, I carried on along quiet lanes flanked by mature oak trees. I wondered again, how, with brutal mechanised hedge cutting, the trees would naturally regenerate. Indeed, a number of these old trees had succumbed to their inevitable fate and remained standing, stripped bare of bark in stark, fantastical shapes, clawing at the sky, only a convenient perch for dismissive birds such as crows or pigeons. As I approached Bobbington, I was continually being pushed aside by large, agricultural tractors and assorted farm machinery, which I didn't mind, especially as I would invariably get a cheerful wave from the driver. However, the downside of this activity is that the narrow lanes were becoming badly damaged, the traffic converging on an establishment in the vicinity of Leaton Hall. I had a brief gander at this bustling enterprise but thought I had better carry on because I imagined my attentions would be unwelcome. My final approach to Bobbington was along Church Lane, where I paused for a while by a field gate looking northwards across to Halfpenny Green airport, becoming aware of light planes and helicopters taking off over my head. This airport was established during the Second World War for the RAF and became a civil airport serving Wolverhampton in 1961.

I arrived back at The Red Lion in good time, so I decided to explore the local countryside in the direction of my travel. I located my car and drove onto Claverley to check out whether the pubs would be open next day. This was not a straightforward endeavour as, after driving through Halfpenny Green, I got diverted by roadworks in Heathton and got hopelessly lost in the narrow, tortuous lanes before Claverley. The small lanes into the relatively large village were also very narrow and difficult to negotiate in a car. Later in the pub, back in Bobbington, locals assured me there was no good road into Claverley. Parking up behind The Crown Inn, I passed through an impressive arch in the centre of an incredible, massive, two-storey, brick-built barn, which, as far as I could see, was not being put to any practical use. It seemed a little strange that such a fine building's only apparent purpose was to allow access to an unmade car park. I'm sure this building would be listed.

I enquired of a smart-looking chap parking up beside me in an equally smart-looking car whether the pub was open. He replied in

The Crown - entrance to car park, Claverley high street © P. L. Chadwick

the affirmative but explained he was more interested in having his hair cut in a shop across the road than imbibing in the pub. From a cursory glance at his head, which appeared to be perfectly well groomed to me, I concluded he must be a little obsessed with his appearance. For a moment I was tempted to join him across the road, to control my own shaggy, unkempt head, with hair almost as long as when I was at university but thought better of it in these challenging Covid-19 times. I have to admit here, as one might easily surmise, that I'm not obsessed with my appearance.

I called into the pub for a well-earned pint and checked with the elderly landlady that she was open the next day. Claverley had that 'time has passed by' feel with attractive black-and-white cottages lining a narrow, sinuous street, difficult to drive through. Therefore, apart from the intrusive traffic and some ugly roadworks outside the pub, which I thought might be intended to improve the sewage situation, this felt like an ancient, unspoilt Shropshire village off the beaten track. In a way I'm not surprised, and felt that it was entirely appropriate, that this village was lived in for a few years by Mary

Whitehouse, teaching at a local school, a campaigner against an antique morality, attempting to hold back the tide of liberalism, a stance that greatly amused and annoyed me in equal measure at the time, in the 1960s and '70s.

After this lunchtime, slightly vicarious, escapade, I returned to The Red Lion in Bobbington for rest and recuperation. Here I spent an agreeable evening eating and drinking at a socially acceptable distance, hugging a distant corner of the bar. I was made very welcome by the brothers running the pub, who showed a great interest in my exploits. Later in the evening, a group of noisy young men arrived in the pub, like a flock of thuggish starlings descending on their roost, paying very little attention to any social distancing rules, effectively ignoring instructions not to stand at the bar and exhibiting a very Trumpian belligerence. Here I have to own up to inventing a new adjective, namely 'Trumpian', inspired by the behaviour of the former American president, which I would define as 'a disregard for expert opinion, amazing arrogance and personal self-aggrandisement. A predilection to exhibit an 'I know best attitude' and an ability to promote fake news in spite of the rational scientific evidence to the contrary'.

These were working men, and I had a sort of empathy with them, experiencing a similar evening gathering of starlings in the bar of my local, The Coach and Horses at Weatheroak in Wythall, just out in the countryside south of Birmingham. I had penned this little tribute, in the style of Dylan Thomas's Sailors Arms in *Under Milk Wood*, to capture that moment, almost imagining the discourse in a Welsh accent. I thought this short verse could equally apply to the gathering in The Red Lion that evening.

> *Grafting geezers gather gratefully*
> *To whet their whistles*
> *Bawdy banter bounces about the bar*
> *In The Coach and Horses.*

This invented adjective, 'Trumpian', I think also applies to the relatively small group of people who refuse to obey the Covid-19 rules of wearing masks in shops and on public transport in this country. In spite of the behaviour of these men, the proprietors, I believe, were grateful of the custom in these depressing days. At times, it was difficult to pass through this throng to get to the gents and, as if to compensate for my discomfort, the proprietors produced a free T-shirt emblazoned with the appropriate Red Lion logo. I gratefully accepted the gift, not knowing whether I would wear it, but it has proved to be very comfortable for walking in, thereby advertising the pub as was clearly intended.

In the morning, as one does, I set off again, towards Claverley. The day was overcast, warm and dry, ideal walking weather. I strolled out of Bobbington along the long, curving street filled with modern infill houses: no doubt a good place to live, but boring to look at. Taking the Boughton Lane, out past the last house, I crossed from Staffordshire into Shropshire. Coming to the junction of a lane, with a nicely trimmed green, I paused before proceeding onto Claverley. I don't quite know why it is, when I come across a junction green in country lanes with a signpost lovingly tended, that my spirits are uplifted. Not that I seriously subscribe to any metaphysical concepts such as spirit, as I'm sure you would expect from my various narratives. Hiking into Claverley, along Church Lane, I thought this lane would benefit visually from the planting of some native trees in the hedgerow, oak or ash probably, as long as they were protected from the ravages of mechanical hedge cutting and the attention of local rabbits.

Coming up to the high street in Claverley, I sat outside the notable church for a while, in a little space called the Bull Ring. I reflected on the observation that this small, ancient village didn't make it as big as Birmingham, with its own famous and much larger bull ring, although they were of the same size in the pre-industrial period. I rested for a while, considering my options. It was early, too early for The Crown Inn to be open, where I had originally envisaged taking lunch. I could have carried on to Worfield, but it seemed a bit of a diversion, however appealing, in my trek around the West Midlands conurbation. I decided, in a moment of clarity, to walk on to Upper Ludstone on the B4176 to The Boycott Arms, having already checked

KINVER TO BREWOOD

Map 07: Bobbington to Pattingham

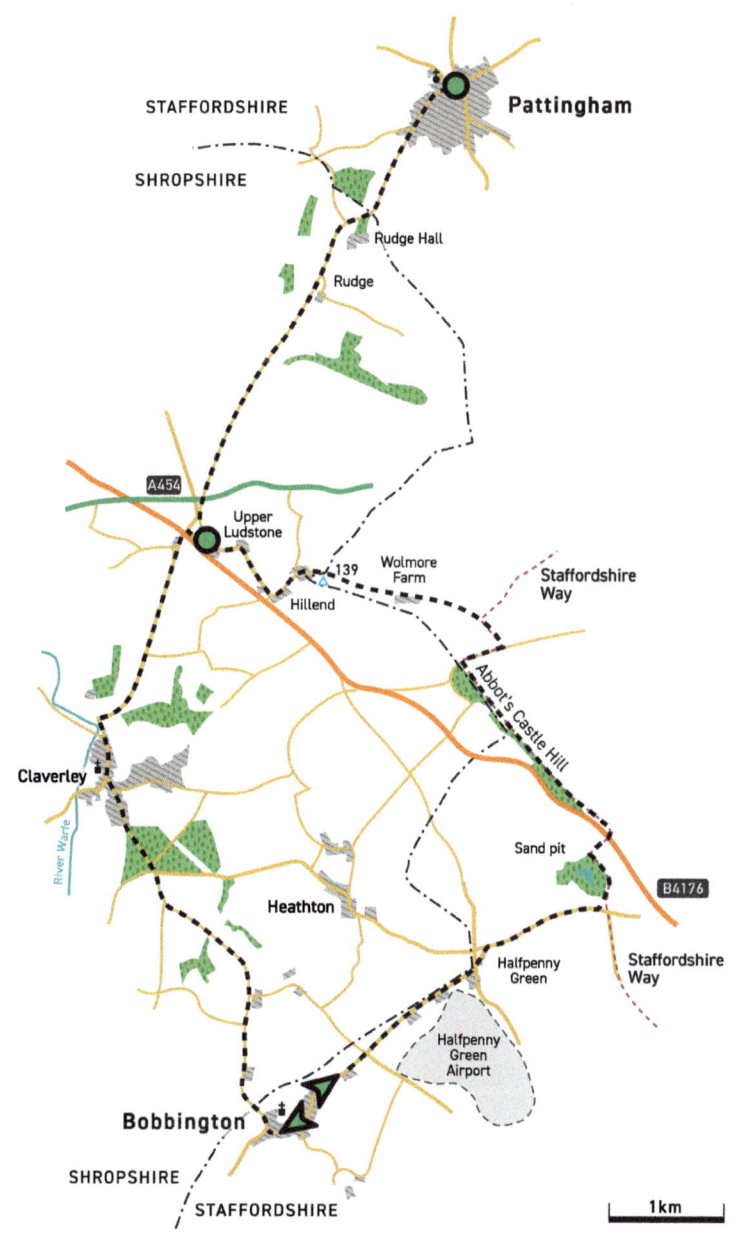

49

Bull Ring, Lychgate, Claverley © *Gordan Griffiths*

with the landlord that they were open for business this lunchtime in these depressing Covid-19 times.

Claverley is one of those places with a confusing road layout, and I had to take considerable care in choosing the right exit. From the church in Claverley, I strolled down the main street past some pleasant dwellings, to a low point of fifty-four metres, before a sharp turn at the bottom of the village. I crossed over a small stream which trundled off to join the River Worfe, whose waters were destined eventually to join the River Severn. I was then faced, as one might expect by the name, with a long climb up to my destination at Upper Ludstone. I asked the way of two chaps out walking their dogs and they said there was a poor footpath, so I trudged up the road through the magnificent sandstone gorge, dripping with native ferns. It was a long, straight climb to Upper Ludstone, past the grounds of Ludstone Hall.

When I arrived at The Boycott Arms, I sat outside for a while, resting until the pub opened, grateful that the day's labours were over. The same two chaps I spoke to earlier in the morning arrived a few minutes after I arrived, pleased and pleasantly surprised that the pub was open. I chatted to the landlord in front of the pub before I was able to successively purchase three pints of splendid Enville real ale, in a carefully organised one-way system. I imbibed on the spacious forecourt, set back from the B4176, the Dudley to Ironbridge Road, before getting a taxi to take me back to Bobbington. I whiled away the evening in The Red Lion, before returning to the big city next morning, determined to resume this trek as soon as possible, Covid-19 allowing.

I returned to Bobbington in early September on the next leg of my clockwise journey around the West Midlands conurbation. I parked up my car, got myself organised and set off for Halfpenny Green. It was a good calm day for walking with the sun breaking through by mid-morning. I strolled out past the local school to White Cross, the first crossroads out of Bobbington. At the junction, there was a large complex of derelict greenhouses. I thought, *what a waste!* I imagined the fun I could have in bringing these back into use, indulging my other main hobby, other than rambling, of growing and selling plants. To my right, I could see the manicured acres of Halfpenny Green

The Boycott Arms at Upper Ludstone © Roger Kidd

Airport with white sheds and mechanical aviation insects dotted around on the immaculate green sward. The small settlement of Halfpenny Green at the northern tip of the airport was well presented with some agreeable cottages. I pressed on past an award-winning vineyard estate, to pick up the Staffordshire Way again, glad to be off the surprisingly busy road. I strolled down the footpath beside an inactive sandpit, brutally scaring the landscape, and trudged up a farm track to the B4176. Reaching the main road, I stood for a while, looking back over the landscape, at this point affording lovely views to the south.

Turning round, I observed the busy road climbing to a height of about 114 metres and reflected on the fact that it was here, many years ago, where I spun my car on a bend at the top of the hill on an adverse camber as the road plunged down the hill. I was driving back from Ironbridge with my family in a Vauxhall Chevette in the 1980s, a car that was notoriously light in the back and therefore liable to skid. I spun the car across to the other side of the road, hitting the soft roadside bank in front of a lorry coming up the hill. The lorry driver was approaching the summit of the hill very cautiously, as though he was prepared for this incident. It was as though he had seen previous accidents on this evidently notorious spot. I waved my appreciation to the driver for his caution and quickly reversed across the road to a refuge on the outside of the bend and took stock of my situation. Luckily, my car was undamaged, and my two-year-old daughter asleep in a car seat in the back did not even wake up. I had wanted to stand on the spot where all this happened and reflect on a lucky escape, but it was further up the busy road, and gaining access to the spot would have been equally as dangerous as the first visit proved to be. Instead, I crossed over the road and kept to the footpath, which, rising all the time, gradually departed from the main road.

Joining the Roman road which traverses Abbot's Castle Hill, I sauntered on through a pleasant oak woodland with silver birch and a verdant fern understory. The busy road groaned on below me as I continued to climb up the hill. Traipsing along through the woodland

View north from Abbot's Hill

edge, there were fabulous views northwards through gaps in the trees of the South Staffordshire countryside, over the land I would be crossing in the coming days. There was a scattering of farms and dwellings in a classic patchwork field landscape of arable pastures and woodland. From this sandstone ridge, the extent of the gently undulating Mid Severn plateau could be clearly seen. Towards the top of the hill, I passed beneath two massive, and no doubt ancient, beech trees, whose significance in this location I could only wonder at. I exchanged pleasantries with a couple out walking locally from the nearby village of Seisdon, who shared my exhilaration at the prospect. This footpath over Abbot's Castle Hill marks the county boundary between Staffordshire and Shropshire.

At the point where the Staffordshire Way meets the lane to Seisdon, at an elevation of 127 metres, there was a house in the form of a mock castle, which I doubt would have named the hill. I did, however, think that the earthworks I thought I had detected adjacent to the footpath were a more likely source for the hill's name. After a short dog-leg down the lane, I picked up a bridleway, which was more like a redundant traffic-free green lane, which propelled me through Wolmore Farm, with its fields of sheep, all the way to Hillend. I stood for a while looking northwards over the gentle undulating plateau and observed the city of Wolverhampton with sentinel blocks of flats high on the skyline to my right. The highest point of Abbot's Castle Hill at 139 metres lies above the attractive hamlet of Hillend. I strolled down the lane towards Upper Ludstone, avoiding the noisy and notorious B4176, to The Boycott Arms, which was, on this occasion, unfortunately shut.

Thus, this was the second time I had walked from Bobbington to Upper Ludstone, the former time being via Claverley. This second perambulation was occasioned by my desire to walk along Abbot's Castle Hill, and I would say the experience was well worth it. If anyone is tempted to follow my circumnavigation of the West Midlands conurbation, they would have a choice of route from Bobbington: either via the atmospheric village of Claverley or via Abbot's Castle Hill. Having reached The Boycott Arms a second time, I was now ready to press on northwards towards Pattingham. Since the pub was closed and I could not slake my thirst, I ordered a taxi to take me back to The Red Lion in Bobbington. As we drove back along the B4176, I could clearly see the sandstone escarpment of Abbot's Castle Hill. We turned off the road at Upper Aston on the way to Halfpenny Green, before the spot where I spun the car. I arrived back at The Red Lion in time for a lunchtime drink, before a luxurious power shower and grateful rest.

Returning next day to The Boycott Arms in Upper Ludstone, I struck out north-eastwards along the straight lane to Pattingham, straight enough to be the remnants of a Roman road. The weather was overcast with a light drizzle which settled on my top in droplets so fine that I was able to brush them off without getting too wet. This could have been a problem if the rain became any heavier because I had, rather carelessly, failed to pack my wet gear in my rucksack, thinking that it would be dry. At the first junction in the lane at the hamlet of

Rudge, I came across a circular stone construction which could only be an animal pound. I discovered later that this medieval construction was in fact a scheduled monument. As I have commented on before, these pounds were used to round up stray animals which were only released on payment of a fine. I strolled on beside the sheep-nibbled grounds of Rudge Hall and crossed over, once again, the county boundary from Shropshire to Staffordshire.

I arrived in the large village of Pattingham early and thought seriously about walking further on. Arriving early now seemed to be a recurring theme, and I thought in my old age that I should be a bit more ambitious in the distance planned to travel. There were two pubs in the village – The Crown and The Pigot Arms – on an old stretch of high street and a nicely prepared green around a notable church. Feeling a bit lazy this day, I sat on a seat opposite a small row of shops and soaked up the atmosphere as the sun threatened to break through the high clouds. I studied the gradual movement of the clouds sinking southwards across the sun, giving occasional, tantalising bursts of warmth. I resorted to inflicting myself on a coffee house in the high street for a socially distanced bacon sandwich and cup of coffee.

Animal pound at Rudge © John M

After a quick squint around the recreation ground, noting the considerable concentration of cyclists buzzing through, I frequented The Crown Inn for my first pint of the day. Sitting in the garden, I mused on the difference between Pattingham and Claverley; the former being clearly historical and claustrophobic with a narrow, twisting, medieval street pattern and the latter, although being an old village, being open and bright with large areas of carefully mown grass. I retired to the handsome Pigot Arms for a couple more pints. Sitting outside while waiting for my taxi to arrive, I was extremely irritated by the unnecessarily elaborate Covid-19 arrangements in this pub, which created large, impatient queues. I returned to Bobbington for rest and recuperation that I did not really deserve, given that I had walked such a short distance this day.

Next morning, a Thursday, I left Bobbington and drove on to the small town of Brewood. I decided to go the long way round, driving back to the A449 at Stourton, and then northwards through Wolverhampton city centre. This was the first time I had ever been to the city of Wolverhampton, admittedly only driving around the ring road. I passed under the M54 and left the trunk road at Coven, crossed over the River Penk and drove into Brewood. I located a free

The Pigot Arms, Pattingham © Philip Halling

car park to the rear of The Red Lion Hotel, my base for the night, off the Stafford Road, and parked up. I changed into walking gear and ordered a taxi in front of the hotel to return me to Pattingham. Only when I pronounced my Brewood location correctly, as used by locals, that is 'brewed', did the taxi driver know where to pick me up.

I strode out of Pattingham northwards, past the village school, and retrieved a soft ball from the gutter hit over the fence by a young lad wielding a tennis racket, to the grateful wave of the teacher in charge. Passing out of the village past roadworks, I climbed again to a height of 160 metres before descending again to 141 metres. This gently undulating road was quite busy and not particularly good walking, but I did have occasion to change maps: from Landranger 138 to Landranger 127. Picking up the so-called County Lane, which unsurprisingly marks the boundary between Shropshire and Staffordshire, I strode up to the A464, the Wolverhampton to Telford road. At the junction, I popped into a pub called The Summerhouse, since, seeing that it had made the effort to open for business in these difficult times, it felt churlish to pass it by. I was to follow County Lane all the way to Codsall Wood.

North of the main road, the narrow, twisting lane was in a parlous state, caused no doubt by traffic gaining access to a curious collection of establishments: an equestrian centre, a dog training centre and an alpaca sanctuary. It was as though the council planners had allowed these non-conforming premises to locate on the very edge of Staffordshire, as though they didn't know where to put them and where they might have thought that it didn't really matter so much. However, today there was little traffic, and I settled into a pleasant stroll, disturbing a group of rabbits in an adjoining open hedgeless field. The damaged lane appeared to be seriously neglected by the local authorities, as though neither was quite sure who owned it, seeing that the boundary passed down the middle of the lane.

Next in my northwards progress, through relatively flat countryside, I reached the busy A41, which I crossed with care. This unremarkable trunk road is in fact the major Roman road called Akeman Street which connects London with Chester. It

A MIDLAND MEANDER

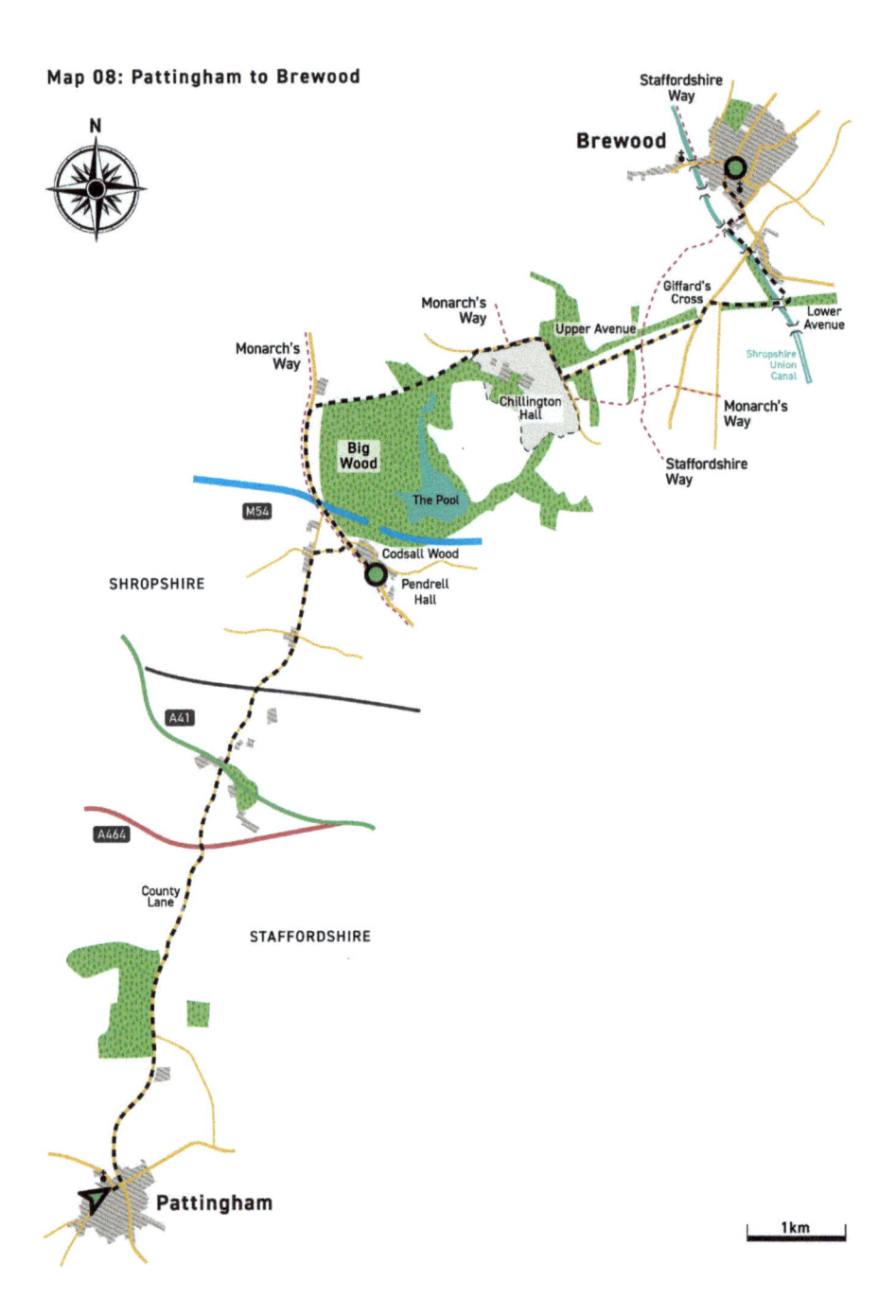

Map 08: Pattingham to Brewood

slices through Birmingham near where I live, where it is called the Warwick Road, and leaves the conurbation after Wolverhampton. We normally think of Roman roads as dead straight, but the A41 Akeman Street in this vicinity may well be the exception, because it is not particularly straight, certainly not as straight as Watling Street further to the north.

Pushing ever northwards, I crossed over the main railway line to Shrewsbury. At the next junction, I was halfway between Albrighton and Codsall, two large, expanded commuter villages with main line stations, between Wolverhampton and Telford. Towards the end of this three-mile lane, I branched off towards Codsall Wood, seeking out the local pub, the historic-sounding Pendrell Arms. When I did reach the pub, I was sorely disappointed. Firstly, because the pub was closed and I couldn't slake my thirst, and secondly, the building was a modern affair in the form of a chalet-type building, with no historic or visual quality. After some research at home, it transpires there is a Pendrell Hall in the vicinity, from which the pub is no doubt named, that is now a college of adult education. However, the hall also has no great antiquity, being built in 1870 for Edward Viles, a Victorian writer of romantic fiction. The popular novel *Black Bess*, which is the name of Dick Turpin's horse, is attributed to this writer who glorified highwaymen, and indeed smugglers, a curious obsession of writers during this time. Even so, there was nothing much of merit in Codsall Wood, being composed of mainly modern houses strung out along a long, straight road. I cut my losses and ordered a taxi to take me back to The Red Lion Hotel in Brewood.

Brewood seemed a pleasant enough small town with a compact, bustling central marketplace. From the outside, The Red Lion Hotel appeared to be a plain, rather drab, Georgian building, hard up against the street, but the inside of the hotel was greatly improved and modernised. As I sat in the bar, sitting by the ample front window with a lunchtime drink, I was able to study the activity in the market square, with its stone horse trough planted up with flowers. The signpost opposite curiously contained directions to the local Catholic school, as though it was a real place of interest. My abiding memory was, however, at breakfast next day, of the traffic chaos caused by a number of massive agricultural machines trying to pass through the narrow market square, in opposite directions, at the same time, each unwilling to give way to the other. In the evening, I had a pleasant meal, albeit a bit close to the next table for comfort. I fell into conversation with a couple on the adjoining table who had hired a canal boat for the first time, as a different and allowable holiday break in these Covid-19 times. Although the chap remained positive about the experience, the woman was not so keen, suggesting that the experience was a little boring, enjoying the walk and meal in Brewood and not looking forward to returning to their berth on the nearby Shropshire Union Canal. For my part I have to empathise with the woman in this case, thinking that canal boating is a somewhat arcane and tedious activity. This is, I think, primarily because, in my opinion, the landscape can be repetitive for many unbroken miles, often with very limited vistas to engage the wandering eye.

Marketplace in Brewood © Roger Kidd

Brewood

> Another small town
> Passed right through
> Like many others
> Before, it's true
> This one patronised by Pugin.

I returned to Codsall Wood in the morning by a taxi which drove much too fast along a narrow, twisting lane off the Brewood to Codsall road just south of the M54. The lane, which would have been good for rambling, passed through the hamlet of Gunstone and past Leper House; I was sure the latter would have some gruesome stories to tell. I think if I owned a house thus called, I would be sorely tempted to change its name. I was dropped off by The Pendrell Arms and proceeded to walk north-westwards, towards the M54. I trekked on beside the big wood, part of the Chillington Hall Estate, marked on its boundary by a distinctive brick wall. The southern extremities of this wood, graced by some very mature trees fronting the road, were sliced off from the main body of the park by the motorway. Just before crossing the highway, I clipped the furthest extent of County Lane that I had been walking yesterday. I crossed over the thoroughfare and strode on northwards past a narrow strip of agricultural land between the road and the back wall of the estate. On this short section I had joined, once again, for the last time, the Monarch's Way.

I found a bridleway skirting the northern boundary of the Chillington Hall Estate and turned significantly eastwards. This was a very satisfying walk of about a mile and a quarter in the morning sunshine along the woodland edge, possibly my favourite place to walk. At various points along this stretch, the brick wall had lost its integrity to the invasive heave of tree roots and the weight of fallen trees. I negotiated a muddy section as the path descended to cross a small stream that fed the large lake, called The Pool, in the estate landscaped by Capability Brown. At the point where the bridleway met the next lane, there was a sumptuous dwelling attached to the hall, modestly called The Gardener's Cottage. Passing the back entrance to the hall, I observed a notice on the locked gate which read 'Covid-19 controlled film set'. Wondering what they were filming, I trekked along the lane beside Horse Paddock Wood and disturbed a red grouse from its cover. Coming up to the main ceremonial entrance to Chillington Hall, I observed the grand house through impressive wrought iron gates and, turning round, the upper tree-lined avenue stretching away to the north-east. Chillington Hall has been owned by the Gifford family since 1178 who, being royalists in the English Civil War, helped Charles II to escape capture after his defeat in the battle of Worcester. The current grand Georgian edifice was, however, built much later, in the eighteenth century.

Striking out along the straight lane beside the upper avenue, I interrogated my map for the Staffordshire Way which cut across this ceremonial tree-lined avenue. I searched very carefully for the footpath on the ground but found no discernible sign of it, therefore concluding that signposts must have been deliberately removed. I carried on up the straight lane to the main road, where I crossed the avenue at Giffords Cross, obviously named after the family owning the hall down the avenue, noting another grand, gated entrance. I took a footpath along the lower avenue all the way to the Shropshire Union Canal. The lower avenue, however, continued further on, right down to the River Penk. The entrance to the wooded walk was a bit knocked about with areas of recently created, brilliantly red ground. I concluded that a sandpit had recently been filled in. My evidence for this was twofold: firstly, there were the remains of tattered ropes adhering to tree branches where kids would have swung out over the abyss, and secondly, from the disgruntled cry of dismay by a pair of mountain bikers recently arrived deprived of the thrill of careering down steep slopes into the former pit. I must admit, from my point of view, I thought these groundworks offered the promise of the woodland returning to a more natural state, deprived of these essentially destructive activities.

I strolled on through the wood graced by extremely mature oak and beech trees all the way to the Shropshire Union Canal, where the lower avenue crossed the deeply cut shady canal by virtue of a grand bridge. This was no mean crossing; on the contrary, it was a wide architectural feature with an elaborate curved stone balustraded parapet on both sides, admittedly in a fairly ruinous state of repair. My surmise is that the two-mile avenue emanating from Chillington Hall was there first, before the canal was built, thus requiring the canal builders to install this monumental construction as a rite of passage. I dropped down to the canal via a precarious unscheduled path and walked on to Brewood. The Shropshire Union Canal is the last major trunk narrow canal built in England by Thomas Telford in 1835. It connects the Midlands canal network – centred on Birmingham via the Staffordshire and Worcestershire Canal at Autherley Junction, north of Wolverhampton – to Birkenhead and the River Mersey.

At the point where the Staffordshire Way is shown on the map to cross the canal, I strode up a track to the main road into Brewood, past a classic water mill with a duck pond fed by a small stream running down to the River Penk. I sauntered up the street past the sandstone church, designed by the famous architect Augustus Pugin in his gothic revival style and built in 1844, to the centre of the large village. As a

Avenue Bridge No.10 © *Matt Fascione*

Catholic, he seemed to be drawn to this part of the country and was responsible for many churches in the area. In the past, Brewood was regarded as a town, reaching a population of 3,799 according to the 1831 census, but lost population in the industrial revolution primarily to the giant city of Wolverhampton burgeoning on its doorstep, seven miles to the south. It was not until the 1950s that the population of Brewood recovered beyond this level.

Before returning to The Red Lion, I called into the second ancient, unimproved pub in the centre of the village, The Sun Inn, for a couple of pints, standing in an out-of-the-way corner of the bar. I observed a group of half a dozen elderly chaps across the lounge, happily engaged in a convivial lunchtime drink. It reminded me of a time I used to undertake a similar activity, in my local, The Coach and Horses at Weatheroak Hill, at a time before my partner retired and demanded more of my time. It also reminded me of how relaxed my father was, engaged in a similar activity, many years before, standing at the bar in The White Hart in Eltham in south-east London, before returning home for a nap and picking up my mother from work. I wonder now whether he told her he had been to the pub? I reflected on the observation that this activity, namely standing at a bar with a pint of beer, may be caused by hereditary considerations.

In the morning I had to return to The Red Lion in Bobbington to repatriate a room key that I had inadvertently failed to hand in when I left. First, I drove out of Brewood to Bishop's Wood, crossing over the Shropshire canal at 'The Bridge'. Here there was some evidence of activity relating to the canal, but my general impression was of a town that largely ignored the canal, although I can't believe that this was an opportunity that would have been missed in the past. From Bishop's Wood I turned southwards and made a brief detour to Boscobel house. This was where Charles II, fleeing for his life, reputedly hid in an oak tree to escape capture. The house was owned by the royalist-supporting Gifford family of nearby Chillington Hall and is, as previously explained, the northern most extent of the Monarch's Way.

Picking up the road beside the big wood, I retraced my steps along County Lane, through Pattingham, all the way back to Bobbington.

After handing back my room key, and declining to accept a cup of coffee, I carried on southwards to Six Ashes, picked up the A458 and drove back through Enville and Stourbridge and on through the Black Country to South Birmingham. I had hoped to continue with my perambulation around the West Midlands conurbation later in the autumn, but the Covid-19 virus took hold

The Royal Oak, Boscobel © Philip Halling

again, with local lockdowns in Birmingham, so I declined further exploration in 2020. Generally speaking, I was relieved that I had at least been able to cover some distance in this depressing, disease-ridden year: a mere twenty-five miles from Kinver to Brewood.

Chapter 3
Brewood to Tamworth

Whoever would have believed that the second autumn lockdown would have dragged on for so long, well into the summer of 2021. After a couple of jabs of the efficacious vaccine, I felt I was ready to go off again in late May. Making my base in The Littleton Arms in Penkridge, I arrived early enough to start walking the same day. I caught a taxi back to Brewood to continue my northwards perambulation. Disembarking in the central square, I took the opportunity to gaze around, soaking up the atmosphere in this small, bustling town. As if to welcome me on my next adventure, the sun burst through the clouds and showered me in warmth.

Setting off in good spirits, I left Brewood via Sandy Lane and strolled out through roads lined with pleasant dwellings, past the lovingly looked-after grounds of the local cricket club. Out in the country, I reached the River Penk, a significant stream originating on the western outskirts of Wolverhampton and flowing northwards to join the River Sow emanating from the county town of Stafford. I stood on the bridge for a while and admired the clear, flowing waters, looking carefully into the stream, but saw no fish. Turning round, I observed the classic conical shape of Brewood on the skyline wrapped around its church with a prominent spire. I slogged up the busy road blighted with traffic, over Clay Gates to the A5, Watling Street, which was in truth not good

Map 09: Brewood to Penkridge

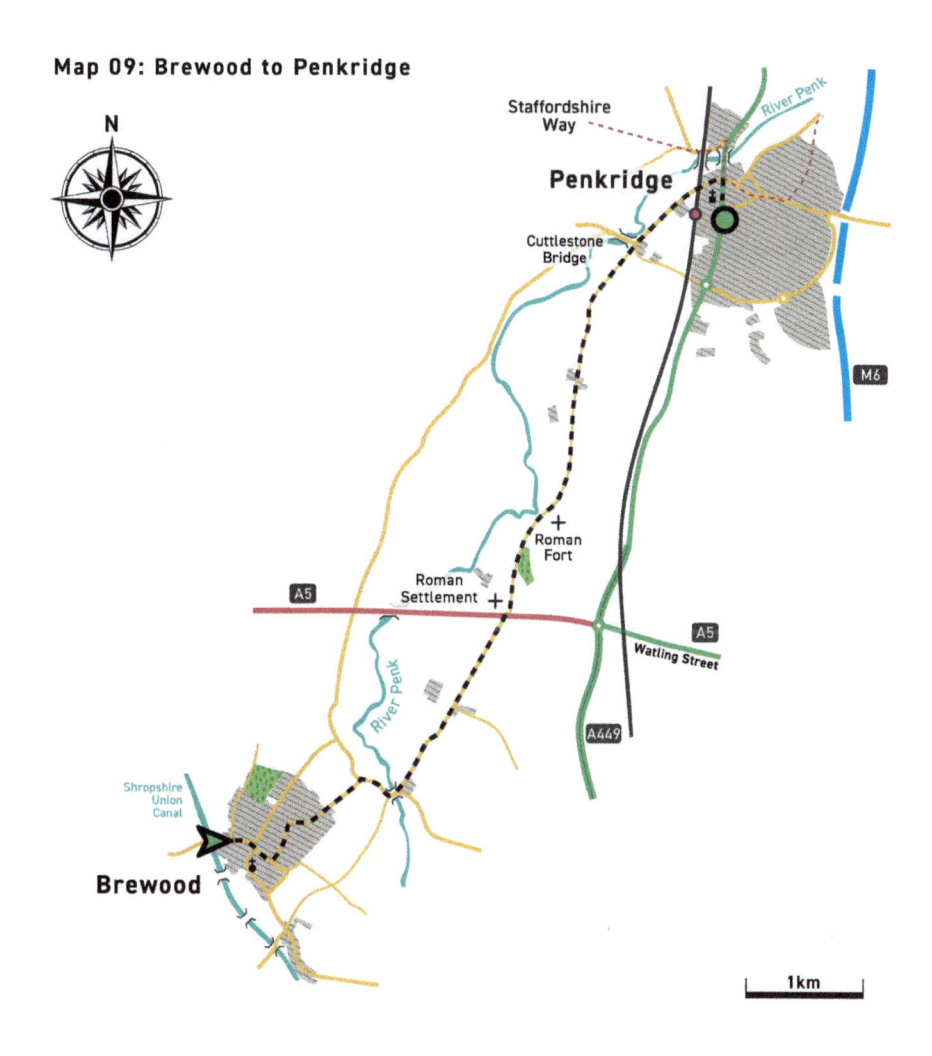

walking. The A5 in this location was also extremely busy, and after a short passage along the verge, I took Water Eaton Lane going ever northwards. To my left was the site of a Roman settlement on Watling Street, that, on careful inspection, I could discern by a small, raised bank in the field. I wondered whether it had been excavated and then buried again, as seems to be the correct procedure in modern archaeological digs. It wasn't hard to imagine Roman legions traipsing up and down Watling Street in this location to quell the unruly Welsh.

The smaller lane was much more enjoyable walking with only the occasional passing car. As I proceeded down the lane, I searched the fields to the east for the site of a Roman fort marked on my map but could only see a ploughed field. I surmised the fort would have been located on the top of the rise to enhance the view over Watling Street, which as far as I could see was dominated by a massive heap of agricultural manure. On the skyline I observed two wind turbines which I presumed were located in the grounds of Rodbaston agricultural college accessed off the main A449 trunk road. This pleasant lane was bedecked by spring flowers: dandelions, buttercups, red campion, sweet woodruff and cow parsley, to name a few. This spectacular display of native wild flowers was rapidly being overtaken by burgeoning swathes of thuggish nettles. Trekking along in the valley of the River Penk, I passed the point where the river appeared, from the map, to touch the lane; although any views of the river were obscured by a dense wood, the lane was graced by extensive puddles and surface running water. A passing motorist considerately pulled over to avoid splashing me with water and asked me if I was lost, which I wasn't, and expressed the sentiment hoping that I wouldn't get too wet passing through. I thought the lane I was travelling along was straight enough to be another Roman road.

I passed a farm that was serving raw fresh milk to the public from the milk shed, and opposite I could buy free-range eggs, though I doubt they were really free. Approaching Penkridge, I passed through the Deanery Estate, which contained a number of very fine dwellings scattered along the lane. Evidently, this estate is derived from a medieval manor that was granted to the archbishop of Dublin by a grateful King John in 1215. I wondered whether there was still an Irish connection. I reached the junction where the road from Whiston coming in from my left crossed the River Penk by the impressive Cuttlestone Bridge, made of massive, red, sandstone blocks. I strolled into Penkridge past its medical centre and under the major north/south main line railway. Coming up to the A449 trunk road opposite a large black-and-white building demonstrating antiquity, I observed a nicely planted-up island off the main road at the junction with Market Street. This trunk road was a major stagecoach route connecting

Cuttlestone Bridge © John M

London and Birmingham to Manchester and Liverpool and linking the county towns of Worcester and Stafford. I arrived in Penkridge about quarter past one, a small town which has always been on an important communications corridor. Sitting outside The Littleton Arms, before checking in, I ordered three pints of Enville ale and some food, reflecting on the fact that the recalcitrant sun was, at last, making an appearance in late May.

After a decent rest, I had a stroll around the town, down Market Street, the original main axis of the town, running from St. Michaels church to the site of the marketplace, showing some older buildings of character. I observed a bowls match taking place on a well-cared-for bowling green in front of the forbidding sandstone church. These sandstone churches stained black appear less like places of enlightenment and more like satanic places of superstition. This observation relates to other places of worship passed on this journey: Hartlebury, Enstone and even Lichfield Cathedral, which I intended to walk past in the not-too-distant future. In Penkridge the newer suburbs stretch away eastwards, over the Shropshire Union Canal towards the M6. After a satisfactory meal in the restaurant, I was allowed to prop up a secluded corner of the bar to while away the evening, involving the bar staff in convivial conversation. One of the thoughtfully masked bar staff mentioned that Penkridge was a favoured stop-off point for people undertaking that classic challenge of walking from Land's End to John O'Groats.

Penkridge

> All is passing through
> Canal, railway,
> Trunk road, motorway
> Staffordshire Way.
> And walkers off to John O'Groats.

In the morning, after a continental breakfast, I shuffled out of Penkridge along Mill Street on the way to the village of Bednall. I paced up the road towards the M6 motorway, passing underneath by means of a dismal tunnel, to pick up the Staffordshire and Worcestershire Canal, the very same canal that I encountered in Stourport, in the early days of this epic journey. The towpath doubled up as the Staffordshire Way. Along this short stretch, I kept up with a canal boat chugging along at walking pace, belching out noxious fumes. I passed a boatyard and a carefully manicured lock facility, before crossing over the canal and passing into the Staffordshire countryside. This was an extremely attractive stretch of country, with some pleasant dwellings, unfortunately blighted by the noise emanating from the nearby motorway.

Taking the well-marked footpath through a field of growing wheat, I passed onto the Teddesley Park Estate. The boundary of the estate was marked by an artificial raised bank containing a small stream, effectively forming a boundary ditch, flowing from the Spring Slade Pool, an unusual landscape feature that I have never encountered before. Teddesley Hall, now long demolished, was once the home of Sir Humphrey Littleton, a local bigwig and MP commemorated hereabouts in the names of local pubs. I strolled through an open landscape, with a massive, ploughed field devoid of any hedgerows,

BREWOOD TO TAMWORTH

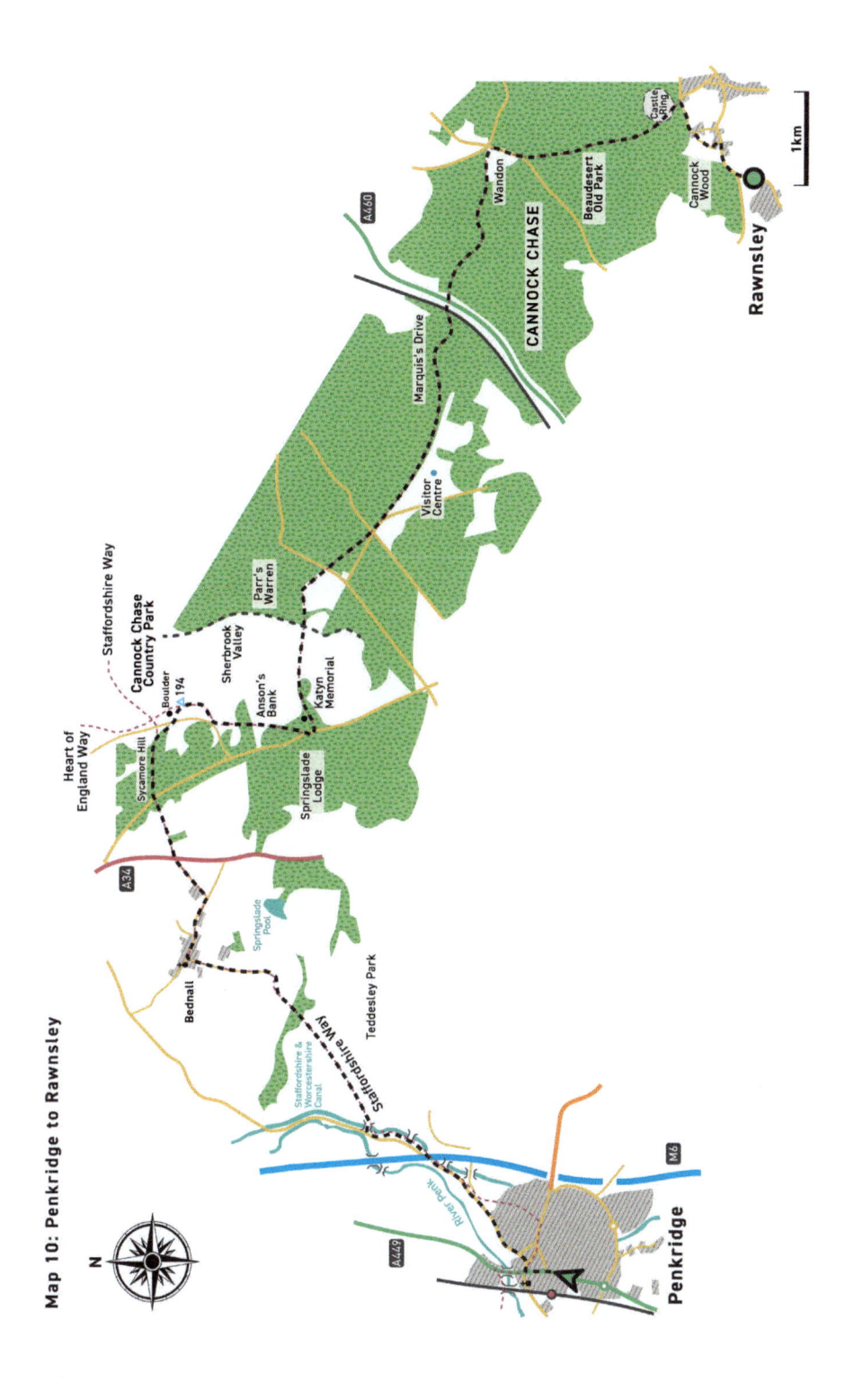

Map 10: Penkridge to Rawnsley

with old, gnarled oak trees dotted around. Some of the trees seemed to be blasted, suffering terminal decline, and I did wonder whether this might be due to the overuse of agricultural chemicals. My impression frankly was of a poorly managed landscape. The gently undulating contours with red soil reminded me of that of south of Penkridge and I did wonder whether I was still traversing the same Mid Severn plateau.

At a high point of 117 metres, I stood still for a while and looked around. To the south I could see the distinctive wind turbines catching the breeze in the grounds of Rodbaston Agricultural college, and to the west, in the far distance, I could see the Shropshire Hills. To the north-east, I could see the spire of Bednall church about a mile further on. Beyond that, I could clearly see Sycamore Hill and the leaden line of evergreen trees on Cannock Chase. Due west, beyond Telford, I could see the distinctive conical hill that is the Wrekin, a dormant volcano, that I have yet to climb.

At this time of the year, the May trees in the hedgerows were in glorious flower. Approaching the most northerly point of this trek around the West Midlands, I followed the Staffordshire Way all the way into Bednall, a pleasant enough small dormitory village without a pub. I came up to another major trunk road, the A34 which connects Southampton to Manchester, slicing through Birmingham very near to where I live. After crossing the road, there was a stiff climb up onto Cannock Chase, and looking back, the path afforded spectacular views of the Staffordshire countryside. I reflected on the perception that this countryside that I had been crossing since Kinver was rather splendid, with a distinctive character. At the dramatic entrance to the wood cloaking the lower slopes of The Chase, I turned round for one last appreciation of the view and spied the Clee Hills to the south-west and the Long Mynd to the west. Cannock Chase is indeed composed of the same Triassic rocks as the Mid Severn Plateau but forms an uplifted block of land. At the point that I was standing to look around, I was directly above the western boundary fault line.

I crossed over busy Camp Lane and climbed to the top of Sycamore Hill, the most northerly point in this circumnavigation. I carried on up to the next lane and heard a cuckoo in the distance. I reached the Boulder, a local landmark, a glacial erratic originally from Scotland, dumped by the retreating ice at the end of the last Ice Age. Nearby, the high point of 194 metres was marked by a trig station. To the east, above the treeline, The Chase opened up to a wide expanse of heathland. Ahead was the deep valley of the Sherbrook, but today I turned significantly south, striding over the Brocton Field, picking up the Heart of England Way, leaving the Staffordshire Way for the last time. To the north-east, with no trees to obscure the panorama, there were stunning views across the bare top towards Rugeley down in the Trent valley. I crossed over Anson's Bank and walked down to the Katyn Memorial. I thought this flower-strewn memorial was much too modest for the appalling atrocities that were committed by the Russian state to the Polish people in the Katyn Forest in the chaos at the end of the Second World War.

I strolled down to the Spring Slade Lodge, a remote café facility on The Chase, and wondered whether it had any connection to the aforementioned Spring Slade Pool. To my dismay, my attempts to

Glacial erratic Boulder Cannock Chase

order a taxi were thwarted by the fact that my phone had run out of juice. So, in desperation, not wishing to entertain the torment of a walk back to Penkridge, I implored the proprietors to kindly order me a taxi, which I am pleased to say they did with exceedingly good grace. When the taxi arrived, in a rickety black cab, the driver, who never stopped talking, regaled me with tales of visiting this very café with his grandmother in his youth out from Cannock for a stroll around the local upland. We drove back to Penkridge, past the pristinely kept German cemetery near Broadhurst Green, across remote and rugged terrain. In The Littleton Arms, I spent another very pleasant evening before packing up in the morning and pausing this perambulation, the first outing in the Covid-19-ravaged year of 2021.

In early July, with the virus taking off again, having been double jabbed, I decided to risk setting off again on another leg of this circumnavigation. I drove to Cannock Wood via Lichfield and parked up in The Rag Country Inn at Rawnsley. Waiting for my pre-booked taxi to arrive, I changed into walking gear. I observed several large tents set up in the grounds, waiting expectantly for hordes of football supporters to watch the unfolding matches in the delayed 2020 European Football Championship on a big screen.

Starting again at the Spring Slade café on Camp Road, I followed the Heart of England Way up past the Katyn Memorial and set off across Cannock Chase. Although overcast, the day promised to be mainly dry. I was aiming for the Castle Ring, an Iron Age hill fort of the south-eastern edge of The Chase. After a short passage through attractive, open heathland, I plunged down into the Sherbrook Valley. To the south of the track, the waters appeared to be gathering in a marshy swamp after heavy rain on the previous days. To the north, the insipient stream trickled down the valley to Shugborough Park before flowing into the River Trent. The eastern side of the valley was clothed in the trees of Parr's Warren, the start of a large, open-access area. Much of this rugged upland is owned by the Forestry Commission and designated as an Area of Outstanding Natural Beauty. The long-distance footpath was a wide, easily followed, stoned track, much loved by mountain bikers.

Katyn Memorial, Cannock Chase © Tricia Neal

I crossed over Penkridge Bank Road and proceeded to the next road junction, whereupon I passed onto another map, Landranger 128. Still following the track, I passed through the Cannock Chase Country Park in an area festooned with poorly parked cars. However, I was quite impressed by the number of people out walking and cycling this day, enjoying the local facilities based around a popular visitor centre. No more than a few hundred yards from the visitor centre, the crowds began to thin and, in a quarter of a mile, disappeared entirely. Only mountain bikers were still buzzing around, enjoying the various rides that the area is famous for. Climbing to a height of 197 metres, I joined the Marquis Drive which snaked down to the transport artery crossing the upland in a deeply cut valley, which contained the railway and the A460 Cannock to Rugeley Road. The original railway crossing appeared to be by surface-level path but now, thankfully, a newer bridge is provided to carry walkers and cyclists across the track. However, no such facility was provided to cross the busy, dangerous road, and I waited for some time to cross safely with a host of impatient cyclists dangerously nudging their front wheels into the road.

I slogged up the hill, out of the valley, under Lower Cliff beside a small stream. Contrary to my initial impression, that The Chase was planted up entirely with conifers, I observed areas of mixed deciduous woodland. Indeed, down in the valley to my left, I saw a patch of distinctly foreign eucalyptus trees. At the next road junction, at a height of 199 metres, I turned significantly southwards through Beaudesert Old Park. Strolling down the hill to the sound of chainsaws emanating from some nearby forestry activity, I came across a small stream issuing from a beautiful, sparkling lake, bedecked with bullrushes, held back by a concreted section of the track. Further on, after negotiating a low bluff, I approached a second stream and was stopped in my tracks by a grey heron standing in the middle of the path. The motionless bird was observing the overflow of water across another concrete shoot, hoping to catch small fish. I had naturally seen herons before, in the distance or flying, but I had not really appreciated how large they were this close up, appearing to stand at least four feet tall. This section of the walk, devoid of flying bikes, was the most enjoyable part of this ramble across Cannock Chase.

On the steep climb up to Castle Ring, I paused and, as is my habit, looked back. I could clearly see the ridge through the centre of the forest that I had been following and the deep valley housing the road and railway. I reflected on the fact that this path across The Chase had made the passage relatively easy, avoiding the necessity to navigate through badly signposted forest tracks. To my right, slipping off to the south-west, I came across a cleared area sporting an amazing display of foxgloves in full, brilliant flower. I peeled off to skirt the edge of Castle Ring, the highest point on this upland at 801 feet and the most distinctive Iron Age hill fort in the West Midlands, dating from around 500BC. This heavily wooded eight-and-a-half-acre ancient monument is difficult to discern to the casual eye but would have once been home to an important Iron Age tribe, enjoying dominium over this part of the Trent valley.

I passed through into the car park, at the top end of Cannock Wood, and observed the stunning view of the conurbation below. To the south-west, I could see the tower blocks in Walsall town centre and, in the far distance, on the horizon, the ridge forming the southern edge of the tilted-up Midland plateau. I noted some attractive cottages in this northern extension of Cannock Wood before walking down a quiet lane to join Ironstone Road. I reached The Rag Country Inn at Rawnsley about two o'clock. Unfortunately, I was too late to order food, so I sat outside with a few pints before turning in and mused on this ten-mile challenging trek across Cannock Chase, the wildest terrain I had encountered so far on this journey. I observed people practising bowls on the nicely prepared crown green at the back of the pub. Crown green bowls, as distinct from flat lane bowls, is endemic to this part of the country, stretching from Birmingham and the Black Country, north through Staffordshire to the Potteries. In my limited experience of playing the game, I would say that it is certainly more varied and interesting than flat lane green bowls, as played enthusiastically by my father down south.

In the evening, after a satisfactory dinner, I got talking to a local chap in the bar. When I had explained the purpose of my visit, he was keen to tell me all about the historical coal mining activities in the area. Immediately to the west of the pub, towards Rawnsley, was the site of the Cannock Wood colliery which closed in 1973. Down the road the prospect village was built in the 1930s to house the miners from nearby pits. To the south, shown as a large blank space on my map, is the Bleakhouse open cast mine which was operational from 1993 to 2000. Coal mining was an important industry in this vicinity at the very northern end of the ten-mile-wide South Staffordshire coalfield, which stretches for twenty-five miles from Stourbridge, through the Black Country and Walsall, to Cannock Wood. The location of the pub on Ironstone Road, and indeed the name of the pub, reflect the transport of iron to the former colliery, mined from Ragstone quarries in nearby Brownhills, to support historic metal bashing industries. Later in the evening, I watched a football match on television, in the postponed 2020 European Championship, when

Italy saw off Spain in a penalty shoot-out. The same fate was to befall England in the following final.

In the morning, I clambered back up Ironstone Road, through Cannock Wood, to Gentleshaw Common, an eighty-six-hectare lowland heath and nature reserve in the care of Staffordshire Wildlife Trust, which really constitutes a southerly extension of the AONB designation of Cannock Chase. I trekked along Commonside Road, past the hamlet of Gentleshaw, with its redundant windmill and attractive, eponymously named pub. I picked up the winding footpath along the edge of the common, all the while admiring the panoramic views to the south-west over the West Midlands conurbation. It was an agreeable walk in the early morning sunshine, still following the Heart of England Way. Taking some small, traffic-free lanes, I came to Cresswell Green. Coming out of this hamlet, I got into conversation with a chap out walking, going the other way. As a walk leader, exuding that air of competent responsibility, he was carrying out reconnaissance for a future walk, before ushering his flock out from Lichfield. I empathised with his dedication and commitment, having done a similar job myself.

I crossed a small stream and climbed up to Hobstone Hill at a height of 138 metres. I was conscious of a marked change in the scenery, with sandstone gorges and narrow, enclosed lanes, representing a transition off the edge of the plateau to another landscape area. At this point I was following a national cycle track and chanced upon a gated road, which wasn't gated anymore, seeing as it had been unceremoniously smashed to one side of the lane by impatient passing traffic. I trudged on past Pipe Hall, picked up the long-distance footpath again and passed down the side of Maple Hayes, an eighteenth-century manor house now occupied by a special needs school, to gain access to the splendid city of Lichfield. Strolling along a wide swathe of a path, in a light shower, on a final, glorious approach to the city, I observed the striking sandstone towers of the cathedral. I crossed over the busy A51, past a well-used allotment site, skirted around a manicured golf course and entered the local municipal park.

BREWOOD TO TAMWORTH

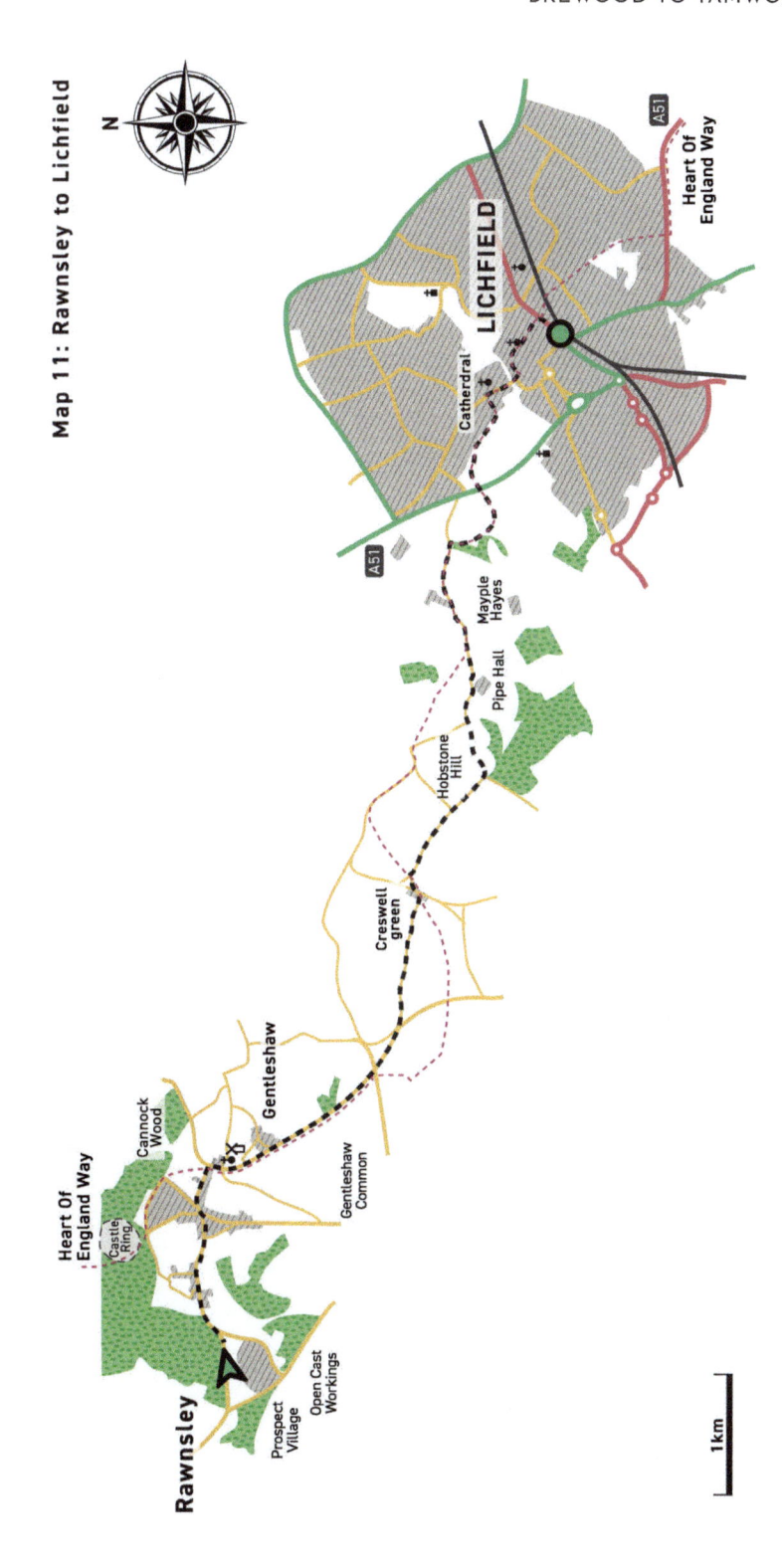

Map 11: Rawnsley to Lichfield

I sauntered triumphantly into Lichfield city centre past Minster Pool, overlooked by the cathedral, at exactly midday. Reaching the main street connecting the town centre with the cathedral, I sat down outside a small coffee shop and consumed a cup of coffee and a bacon sandwich. There was a plaque on a house wall directly opposite which amusingly read 'on this site September 5th 1782 nothing happened'. I sat for a while, people watching, and mused on the fact that Lichfield is probably one of the best organised places one could imagine. An almost perfectly compact settlement of about thirty-four thousand people contained within main roads on the edge of town. A pedestrianised street, leading from the cathedral past the town centre with its market, ushers one up to a new shopping precinct with multistorey parking. An elegant, small city with a wealth of historical associations, which I won't bore you by mentioning here.

After a short rest, I made my way up to the new precinct and located the railway station, where I secured a taxi to take me back to The Rag at Rawnsley. In the evening in the bar, I risked getting into conversation

Minster Pool, Lichfield © Derek Voller

with a grafting geezer, whetting his whistle before going home, who confessed he had no time for hobbies. I advised that he had to find some to keep himself sane, and I informed him that in retirement I had four hobbies, namely: growing and selling plants, walking and writing books about walking, politics and golf. He said he would think about it if he could survive a court case which could cost him a lot of money. This of course would mean, if he lost, that he would have to graft harder and have even less time for hobbies. He seemed to be in a somewhat febrile state, and I worried in a slightly distracted manner about his future prospects and his fragile mental health, selfishly hoping he would not latch onto me for the rest of the evening.

In the morning, after a satisfactory breakfast, I drove on to Tamworth, parked up by my next base, The Globe Inn, and caught a taxi back to Lichfield station. I walked out along the A51 and, just after Cricket Lane, picked up the Heart of England Way again, which would propel me ever further south. The long-distance footpath followed the towpath of the now disused, seven-mile-long Lichfield Canal, which originally connected the Coventry Canal to the Wyrley and Essington Canal, part of the Birmingham navigations, just to the south of Brownhills. I passed two chaps painstakingly cleaning old bricks which were recycled from the redundant canal lock, a very therapeutic activity. The older chap explained that they were in the process of restoring the canal on behalf of the Lichfield & Hatherton Canals Restoration Trust, an activity that had been going on for decades. They were removing a lock, brick by brick, with the intention of lowering the channel under Cricket Lane and building a new lock on the other side. A mammoth undertaking indeed for voluntary labour! I complimented them on their endeavour and wished them well. I was slightly surprised that this important landscape feature was not shown on my ordnance survey map, given that these maps show disused railway lines.

I followed the reclaimed towpath round the canal bend and hobbled up to the A51, crossed over the thunderous A38 and proceeded down the busy road past a redundant pub. Today I was making slow progress, having to mince along because of the arthritic pain in my

A MIDLAND MEANDER

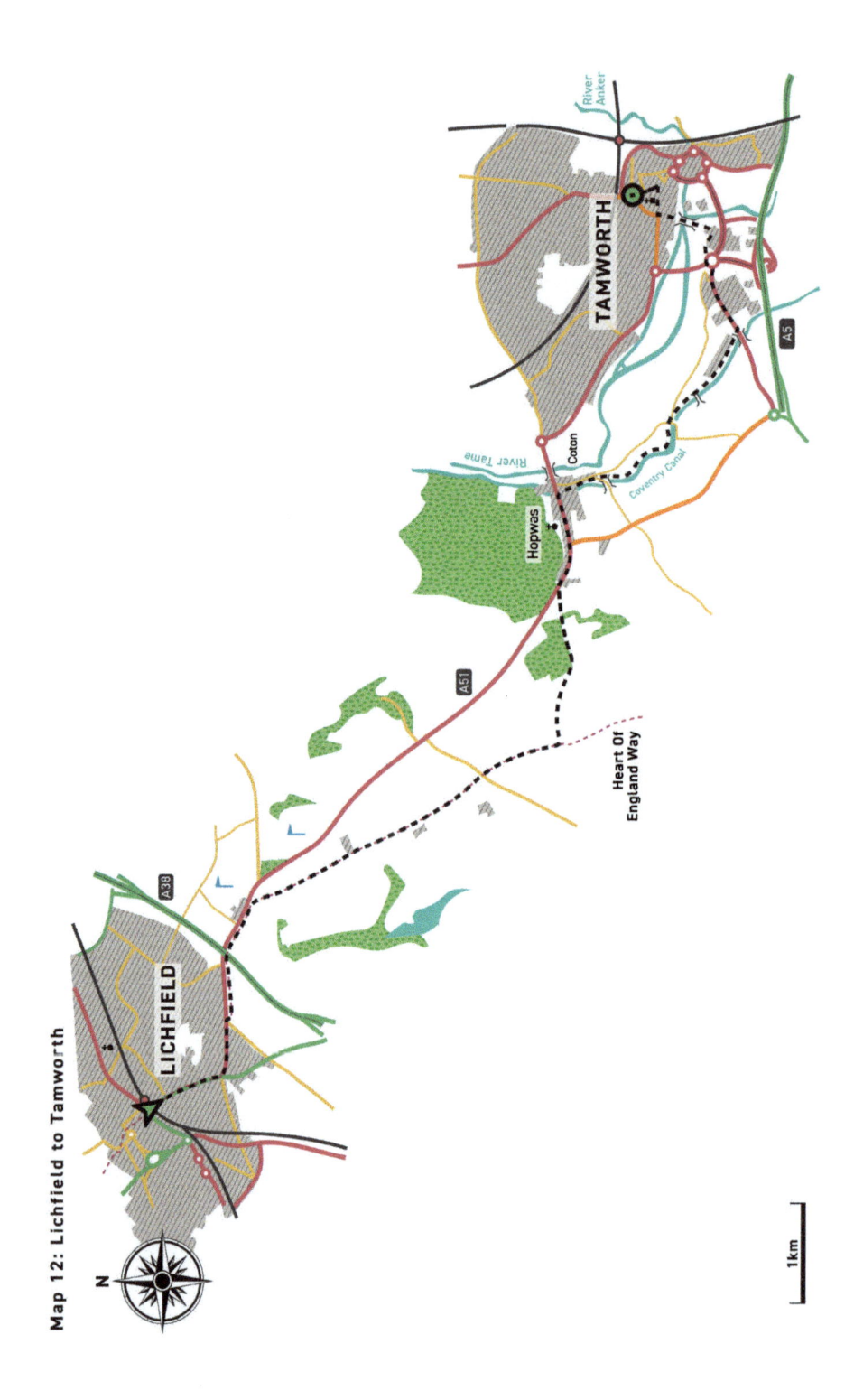

Map 12: Lichfield to Tamworth

right hip. In circumstances like this, I have often found that the pain wears off after a few miles. Looking back to Lichfield, I could see the many prominent spires of the cathedral and parish church against the backdrop of Cannock Chase. Further down the A51, the Heart of England Way departed company with the road to the right, at the point where I passed from Landranger map 128 to 139. I was now faced with a long, straight trek across open countryside along a clearly presented footpath. I passed a field of recently harvested wheat, with the straw being stacked with manure at the field's edge, presumably to make compost. This proved to be an abundant source of insect life for the benefit of numerous birds, notably house martins and grey wagtails, which were swirling around in great numbers, feeding on the insects in flight. I have often fantasised about doing something similar myself, given my other hobby of growing and selling plants and the fact that compost is now becoming difficult to get hold of and rather expensive. This is primarily because the use of peat is rightly being phased out in 2022 because of the destruction of valuable peat deposits which hold carbon dioxide and help to control global warming.

Further on, along the long, straight track, after crossing a quiet lane, I chanced upon a massive pig farm. Here were bare, muddy fields and shallow, trampled hollows and spaced-out piggeries sporting thousands of pink, free-range pigs. It would be a pleasing thought that these sturdy creatures were in fact the famous Tamworth breed of pigs in their rightful place, but this is unlikely because this breed is now distinctly rare. I watched a swineherd usher these cumbersome animals down an ungrazed, electric-fenced track, with loud, piercing shouts, to another section of the field. Hopefully, they were not destined for the abattoir. This long, straight footpath was quite wide in parts, allowing a swathe of wildness, even though the trodden path was a narrow tread. I reached the point where two paths crossed and left the Heart of England Way, turning east towards Hopwas. Following an oak-tree-shuttered path, with an active gravel pit to the south, I came down to the A51 again. I ambled down the hill past smart dwellings into Hopwas, an ancient village where the A51 crosses the River Tame

The Red Lion, Hopwas © Alan Murray-Rust

and the Coventry Canal. I called into the first pub, The Red Lion, for a couple of pints and something to eat. This was the fifth Red Lion that I had visited on this journey and testament to the fact that this is the commonest pub name in England.

Leaving this Victorian brick edifice of a pub, I passed the second colourfully named pub, The Tame Otter, and picked up the Coventry Canal by a very humped humpbacked bridge for a road as important as the A51. Plodding on southwards towards Tamworth, I observed that the generously wide canal in this location is lined with houseboats. Curiously the Landranger map 139 labels the canal here as the Birmingham & Fazeley Canal which is, amazingly for the Ordnance Survey, incorrect. I had intended to get off the canal at Dunstall Bridge and take the small back lane into Tamworth but found the road closed at Dunstall Farm by a massive new housing development, sprawling out over slightly higher ground bordering the floodplain. I wondered about the legality of this road closure and the wisdom of building in this location so close to the floodplain. I was forced to return to the canal which I followed down to the busy A453, one of the main means of vehicular access to the town from the south. I approached the urban centre through an industrial area, along a hectic road with many functional roundabouts. From the last interchange, I took a quiet lane to gain access to the pedestrianised Lady Bridge, the original historical bridge across the River Tame. Walking across the bridge, I admired the extensive water meadows, overshadowed by five tower blocks to the west and a massive sandstone castle crowning a steep mound to the east. I had never been to Tamworth before and had, sitting in my study, often imagined a leisurely stroll across this ancient bridge into the historic heart of the town.

I ambled down Market Street and George Street just as a market was packing up for the day, with its distinctive litter spread around, and then up Coleshill to Lower Gungate Street where my hotel for the night was located. In this north part of the town centre, I have never seen so many places to eat and drink, a facility that presumably has grown up to service the large population of eighty thousand plus in this greatly expanded town with sprawling suburbs to the north-west

Lady Bridge, Tamworth © *Humphrey Bolton*

and south-east; a new town which was never called such. The contrast between this town and the carefully managed outwards development of the city of Lichfield could not be more marked. Tamworth is at least as an ancient a settlement as Lichfield but appears to downplay this heritage. Apart from the part of town around the castle, there is little evidence of the town taking advantage of this fact. In the evening, I treated myself to a Chinese meal across the road from The Globe Inn and spent a pleasant enough socially distanced evening in the pub.

Tamworth

> *Much expanded town*
> *Beside the Tame*
> *Wet meadows around*
> *Lady Bridge fame*
> *Where the kings of Mercia reigned supreme.*

Chapter 4
Tamworth to Alvechurch

In the morning, after breakfast, I made my way back to the impressive Lady Bridge via an ample, if somewhat untidy, church precinct and got myself organised in the gardens at the base of the impressive sandstone castle. The castle is a Grade I listed Norman building, sited at the mouth of the River Anker at its confluence with the River Tame, with a turbulent history. Originally, it was the seat of the Anglo-Saxon kings of Mercia but was successively sacked by Vikings and Danes. Rebuilt by the Normans, it is now one of the best-preserved motte-and-bailey castles in England. During the English Civil War, it was sacked by the parliamentarians in 1643. Even J.M.W. Turner got in on the act and painted a panoramic view of the castle in 1832. More recently, the castle was bought by the local authority and preserved for the nation. The thirty-one-mile-long River Anker, that helps to create the riverine confluence beside the Lady Bridge, originates, after flowing through the centre of Nuneaton, in the Leicestershire countryside between Nuneaton and Hinckley.

Standing again on the pedestrianised bridge, I admired the flowing waters, wide and shallow in this location. I thought this prospect was almost on a par with Stratford-upon-Avon, albeit missing the tourists and canal boats. Tamworth, in spite of its long history, is relatively prosaic, lacking any pretentions, which is surprising given that it

A MIDLAND MEANDER

Map 13: Tamworth to Bodymoor

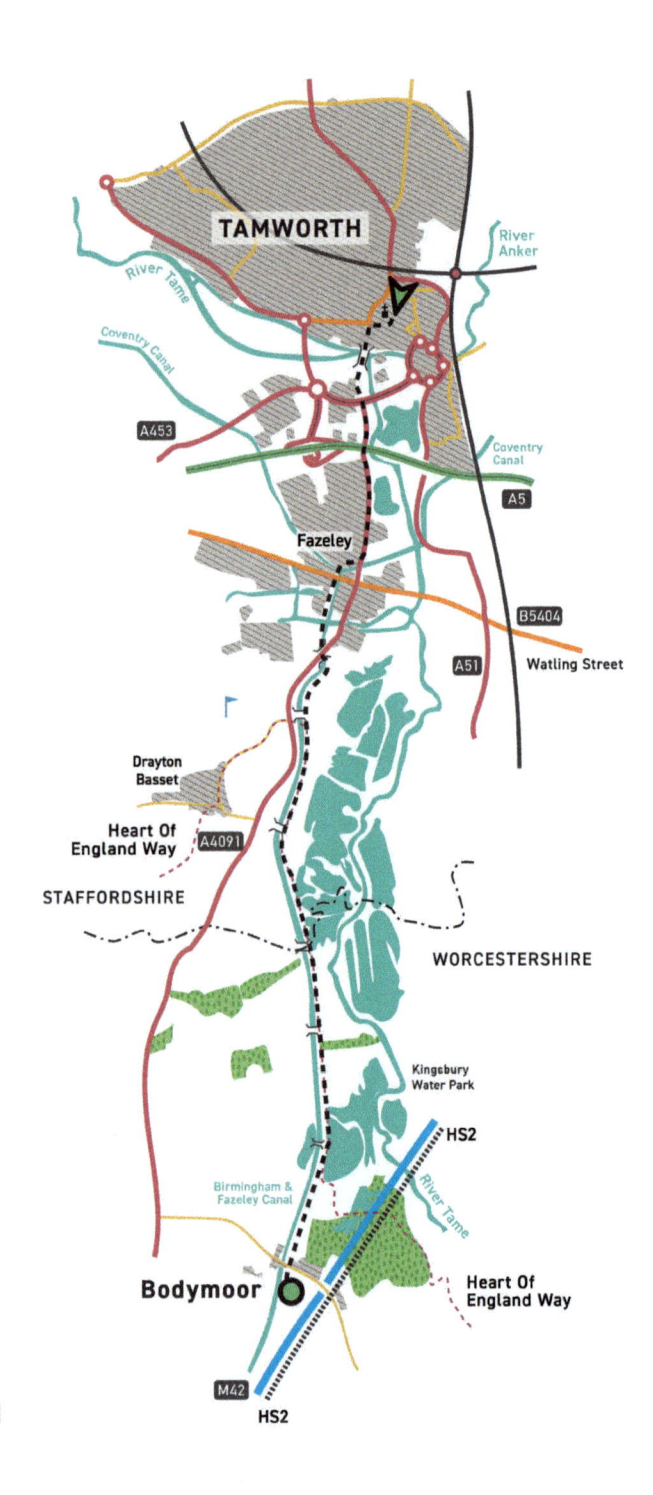

Tamworth Castle from Lady Bridge © Martin Richard Phelan

was the ancient capital of Mercia where the kings of Middle England reigned supreme. I reflected on Roy Fisher's poem *'Birmingham River'* which charts the course of the Tame from its origins in the Black Country. The river passes my old university in Perry Barr, before winding its way through Witton and out of Birmingham via Minworth, turning north to Tamworth and its confluence with the River Trent. Passing under the busy A435 and the A51, I strolled out southwards along a raised bank designed to contain the river waters in times of flood.

I trekked down the A4091 through the northern suburbs of Fazeley until I reached the Coventry Canal. After a short stretch along the canal, ambling to the west, I reached the atmospheric Watling Street junction with the Birmingham & Fazeley Canal. The junction was bedecked with that distinctive canal architecture of warm humpbacked brick-built bridges to carry the towpath over the canals on a scale just big enough to allow the passage of narrowboats. I sat for a while transfixed, observing several boats simultaneously negotiating the sharp bends, amazed at the skill, or lack of it, of the handlers. Before passing on, I popped my head up to the main road through Fazeley, the original A5 Watling Street no less. Pausing for a while, and looking around, I was not surprised by the unprepossessing prospect. I guess Fazeley would have once been a place of importance

Fazeley Junction © *Rob Farrow*

in the seventeenth century, with its canal crossing Watling Street, but today, bypassed, it appears a bit down at heel at the southern extent of the Tamworth urban area.

Pressing on southwards, along the towpath, I passed many moored boats in various states of repair. Some were being used as houseboats, bedecked with plants, rather than canal-worthy vessels. I marked my progress along the canal by a succession of curiously named bridges. I passed under them in order: Tolson's footbridge, Coleshill Road bridge, Drayton Manor swing bridge and Drayton footbridge. This latter bridge, almost a folly, was a curious affair, the like of which I had never seen before. It took the form of two diminutive castellated towers with steep, narrow stairs leading to a precarious narrow span across the canal. Although I'm not particularly fat, I couldn't imagine getting up those stairs without being securely lodged, embarrassingly stuck halfway up. In all honesty, it looked distinctly unsafe. I settled into the long haul southwards along the fifteen-mile, generously wide,

Drayton footbridge, Drayton Bassett, Staffordshire © Roger Kidd

Birmingham & Fazeley Canal, which, passing through level terrain, was open and fresh to the sky, affording splendid views across the surrounding countryside. Further on, I reached Fishers Mill Bridge which also marks the county boundary between Staffordshire and Warwickshire. I passed a lone fisherman on the canal bank so rapt, concentrating on his float, that he didn't even notice my passing. To the east, adjacent to the River Tame, were large areas of open water created by gravel extraction, the RSPB Drayton Lakes. The next bridge was indeed appropriately named Gravel Pit Bridge.

At the Kingsbury Swing Bridge, I paused, taking a brief diversion into the Kingsbury Water Park, renowned for its birdlife, which consists of fifteen lakes in over sixty acres of country park. Coming back to the towpath, I passed a chap running the other way, who responded to my greeting of good morning with an 'alright'. At this point, I knew I was getting close to Brummie land where this greeting is endemic. Next, I reached the first lock on the rising canal climbing up onto the Midland plateau. Finally, I reached the Bodymoor Heath Bridge where I left the canal and searched out a small lane that gave access to The Dog and Doublet Inn. However, I later realised that I could have reached this pub by keeping to the towpath. This old, unimproved, multistoried, atmospheric canal-side pub reminded me of The Angel Inn at Stourport on the River Severn. I spent a very satisfying lunch break in the pub eating and drinking, sitting out beside the restful canal, before the friendly bar staff ordered a taxi to return me to Tamworth. I spent another socially distanced night in The Globe Inn before returning to South Birmingham.

After driving to Meriden, and parking up in my next venue, The Bulls Head, I caught a pre-ordered taxi to whisk me away back to Bodymoor Heath. Once again, the taxi driver wanted only to talk about Aston Villa football club, whose training ground is on the heath. I didn't mind this at all, as it's my club too, but I struggled to keep up with his in-depth knowledge of the players, past and present. I set out along the canal towpath again, under a couple more humpbacked bridges and past another lock lifting the waterway. At the third bridge, I left the Birmingham & Fazeley Canal for the last time. Crossing over the nearby M42 by another footbridge, I ran slap bang into construction works for the new HS2 railway line. I was herded through these works by a rough track enclosed between metal fences. I passed a gaggle of construction workers in white hard hats, pouring over paper plans, so I guessed they must have been managers, rather than persons actually doing the digging. I plodded on down the track to the village of Marston, past a vast field of standing sweetcorn. I understand that the majority of sweetcorn grown as a field crop is used for animal feed.

Coming into the village, I paused by a paddock housing a menagerie of domesticated animals, including two tame pigs that charged over to greet me. The village itself, which is located on the banks of the River Tame, appears to consist of mainly modern houses, but I may have missed the centre of the village. I regret now not having made a slight diversion to have a look. The lane out of Marston, towards the A4097, was blocked, now reduced to an overgrown path, effectively protecting

Map 14: Bodymoor to Shustoke

the village from through traffic. I crossed over the main road and carried on along the very untidy Haunch Lane and on to Lea Marston. There were large areas of apparently disused wetland given over to horse-grazing pasture, running down to the River Tame. Here, the once-proud pavement, past the very posh Lea Marston Hotel, was overgrown with vegetation. Obviously, the local North Warwickshire council were not too keen on clearing this path, or maybe they had just run out of money, or more likely their appointed contractors were trying to save money.

In the compact village of Lea Marston, I lingered for a while on the small village green and observed a well-looked-after telephone box and an elaborate community noticeboard devoid of notices. I picked up the Birmingham Road, joining the Centenary Way to Whitacre Heath. Passing a roadside plot that was being landscaped as a community woodland, I got chatting to a local chap planting trees, demonstrating a gratifying community spirit. He suggested I might like to come back in a year's time and observe the fruits of their labours. Just past the entrance to the Lea Marston purification lakes, I reached the wide and languid River Tame again, set in wet, low-lying water meadows. Next, I crossed the main railway line by a high, arching bridge, which, from the top, afforded a bird's eye view of the Tame's watery meadows and stunning views to the north and north-east over the North Warwickshire countryside.

Plodding on along the lane, I passed the large Whitacre Heath Nature Reserve running down to the River Tame, managed by the Warwickshire Wildlife Trust. This forty-four-hectare reserve consists of pools, woodland and wet grassland and forms part of the Tame Valley Wetlands, a vital north-south migration route providing essential resting and feeding places for thousands of migrating birds. Still walking on a roadside pavement of the Birmingham Road, suggesting this lane was once of more importance, since presumably it went to the big city, I made my way to Whitacre Heath. I observed a sign announcing the start of the parish of Nether Whitacre, an ancient settlement recorded in the *Domesday Book*.

In Whitacre Heath, still following the Centenary Way, by a large roadhouse, I crossed over the next railway. On the far side of the railway, I found a footpath going due south, the combined Centenary and Heart of England Ways. After a short distance, the two paths diverged, and keeping to the Centenary Way, I mused on the enigmatic poem, '*The Road Not Taken*' by Robert Frost, clearly expressing the sentiment that I sadly shared, namely 'I doubted if I should ever come back' and walk the Heart of England Way from this point. I noted another long-distance walk signposted as the 'North Arden Trail', which I guess is a newer addition to the pantheon of such walks in this area since it was not shown on my old Landranger map. Then I passed into Colin Teall Wood, gifted to the parish of Nether Whitacre in 1995 by the aforesaid.

I sat for a while on a convenient bench, also dedicated to this gentleman, affording carefully choreographed easterly views out over the fields towards Hoggrill's End, a curiously named hamlet, which, as suggested by Frost's poem, my boots would never grace. I did wonder, though, whether the inhabitants of this hamlet were inclined to barbecue. Also, I have noticed on my travels many places ending in 'end' which normally indicates a diminutive settlement attached to another with the same first name. Another fine example is Lickey End, lying beneath the Lickey Hills, and the larger settlement of Lickey, close to where I live in South Birmingham. On seeing a sign for Lickey End, two friends from Newcastle were convulsed with laughter, making veiled references to the practice of fellatio or cunnilingus. One of the pleasures of pausing in the headlong rush of a walk is to sit and rest and let the mind wander away. I doubted whether Colin Teall had any such thoughts, but one never knows.

Pressing on through the narrow strip of woodland hard up against the north/south railway, I came to a point where the surface crossing, across another massive railway line coming in from the east, was securely closed. My map showed the Centenary Way crossing the railway line at this point, but given the width of the tracks here, marking it out as a main line, I guess it would be a dangerous surface crossing, thankfully shut. Thus, I was diverted eastwards to cross the railway by a rarely used bridge, and if I had known about this diversion beforehand, I could have enjoyed Hoggrill's End anyway. Hiking through damp, uncultivated, wild meadows, on a slippery track, I skirted around the western end of Shustoke Reservoir. I crossed the River Bourne, a small stream feeding the reservoir upstream and joining the River Tame, just downstream from the major confluence with the combined waters of the Rivers Blythe and Cole, running out of the south edge of the conurbation.

Then, I clambered up the steep, slippery retaining bank of Shustoke Reservoir and sat for a while admiring this attractive stretch of man-made water. The grassy containing banks were being used by locals for exercise and walking dogs, and there were sailing boats on the water. The reservoir used to supply drinking water to Birmingham before the completion of the Elan Valley supply from Wales; it now serves the needs of Coventry and Nuneaton. I pondered on the verdant sward containing the reservoir, doubting that it could actually be mowed. I thought maybe it was kept in this condition by sheep nibbling, but I could see no flock. On further reflection, I thought it more likely that the rise and fall of water in the reservoir, keeping the banks periodically inundated, would be sufficient to produce this effect.

Gaining access to the village of Shustoke via a large car park serving the recreational purposes of the reservoir, I came up to the B4114. I strolled into the centre of the ancient village, admiring the prospect of The Plough Inn, nicely set off behind a small village green. After eating and drinking in the busy pub, which was joyfully disregarding any Covid-19 precautions, I returned to Meriden by taxi. I spent a rather impersonal night in this inn, with the most curious billing arrangements. I normally prefer to set up a tab behind the bar to cover everything, but this was apparently against house rules. My accommodation, food and bar bills all had to be paid separately, causing some confusion and inconvenience. Sitting at the sanitised bar, making polite conversation with the staff, was definitely not allowed, so I had to sit in an out-of-the-way corner with no one to talk to. The pub seemed geared up to cater for groups of people sitting around tables, with no thought of how to accommodate a lone traveller and drinker.

Next morning, a pre-ordered taxi returned me to The Plough Inn, Shustoke. I elected to take the long, straight road south to Maxstoke, which in truth was not particularly safe walking, with the passage of frequent speeding traffic taking advantage of the dead straight road. I noted again that the most common field crop in these parts on light red soil was still sweetcorn. At a high point of eighty-five metres, I leant on a field gate and observed the view westwards to Coleshill with its prominent church spire in the distance, towards a major traffic corridor around the east side of the West Midlands conurbation. I could still hear the insistent hum of traffic from the motorway which had never really left me for the last couple of days. I passed by the entrance to the strictly privately owned Maxstoke Castle, which

TAMWORTH TO ALVECHURCH

Map 15: Shustoke to Meriden

evidently is a fine example of a medieval moated and fortified manor house dating from 1345, open to the public on one day in the year only. I guess this arrangement allows the owners, opportunistically, to take advantage of some heritage grant. Travelling through this essentially flat landscape, I could clearly see the bald dome of Packington Hill on the other side of the River Blythe, a man-made hill of domestic rubbish from Birmingham which closed in 2015. Whilst I'm sure the operators of this landfill site are very proud of their creation, for me it remains an unnatural carbuncle in the landscape.

In the small village of Maxstoke, I passed a ruined priory converted into domestic property. I sat on a bench on the corner by the church and consumed a bar of chocolate and a can of cider. Carrying on, under the M6 motorway, I passed the very popular Forest of Arden Hotel and Country Club, which also contains the Forest of Arden golf course. I remember trying to play this challenging course once, when I was much younger, being totally overwhelmed by its severity, losing many golf balls in the process. With the amount of traffic going to and from this leisure complex, the remaining stretch of this road into Meriden was dire walking. With hindsight, I might have been better taking the Heart of England Way from Church End east of Shustoke, all the way to Berkswell further south, but I would not have passed through Meriden as I desired. So, I had no choice but to slog on along the busy road, with stretches having no grass verge on which to hop onto. Although I am well practised in this art of hopping onto grass verges to avoid oncoming traffic, I would not recommend it to any amateur fellow walker. When I come across a stretch of busy road with no verges to escape onto, I always break into a trot to minimise the possible dire consequences of confrontation with a passing vehicle. Next, I reached the entrance to Packington Hall, another notable stately pile in this North Warwickshire countryside. The prevalence of such stately homes in this area at least matched that observed in the South Staffordshire countryside.

As I approached a farm complex called The Dairy Farm, I noticed that the roads, not shown on my old, rapidly disintegrating map, had been reorganised. I crossed over the A45 by another high, arching bridge and was able to pick up a truncated lane right into the centre of Meriden, a large village which is somewhere near the centre of England. It was a pleasant enough stroll into the village centre, through a residential penumbra, and it was a relief to get off the busy north/south straight road that I had been negotiating since Shustoke. Coming into the village, I sat for a while on the long village green, relaxing and observing the busy scene, consuming pie and chips, conscious that another leg of this marathon journey was now complete. I had a look at the striking memorial, which famously commemorates cyclists who died in the First World War. Finally, I strolled down the road to The Bulls Head for a well-earned rest. In the evening, I sat out another impersonal evening before pausing the journey.

Meriden

> A large village green
> Good place to sit
> Dead cyclists remembered
> Duck pond exit
> Somewhere near the centre of England.

Cyclists War Memorial, Meriden © *Keith Williams*

In late October I prevailed upon my partner to drive me back to Meriden to start another leg of this circumnavigation. From The Bulls Head in Meriden, I carried on down the B4012 to the original centre of this large village, graced by a healthy-looking duck pond supporting a wide range of birds, created by damming a small stream running down to the River Blythe. I'm sure this splendid ornithological spectacle could only be achieved by active feeding of the wildlife present. I took the long, straight lane going due south to Berkswell. After a steep climb out of the village, I observed a sign for the Millennium Way which was not shown on my map. This got me thinking that this long-distance path, which appeared to pass through Meriden, may have been a better option than my chosen route. However, with no guidance from my faithful map, I decided just to slog on due south to Berkswell. In moments like this, gathering the available information, one makes a decision, not knowing if it's the best. Thereafter, one gets dragged into further consequences, which may lift one out of, or bury one further in, the mire, making the situation much worse. At the top of the rise, I paused and appreciated the view westwards towards the Midland plateau with cumbersome planes overhead sinking down to Birmingham Airport.

Further on after the hamlet of Four Oaks, I paused again at a high point of 131 metres and gazed westwards to Birmingham on the horizon. This is pleasant rolling countryside, with old oak trees adorning hedgerows much in evidence, which would have once been part of the far-reaching Forest of Arden. This extensive ancient woodland once reputedly stretched from the River Avon to the River Tame and was defined by three Roman roads – Watling Street, Fosse Way and Icknield Street – and the ancient salt road from Droitwich to the south. The Roman legions evidently preferred going round this dense, impenetrable woodland than ploughing through it. This large tract, part of north-west Warwickshire and the West Midlands metropolitan area, now contains the large cities of Birmingham and Coventry and Solihull and many smaller towns and villages, some of which, such as Henley-in-Arden, Tanworth-in-Arden and Hampton-in-Arden, whose names bear testament to this association.

TAMWORTH TO ALVECHURCH

Map 16: Meriden to Kingswood

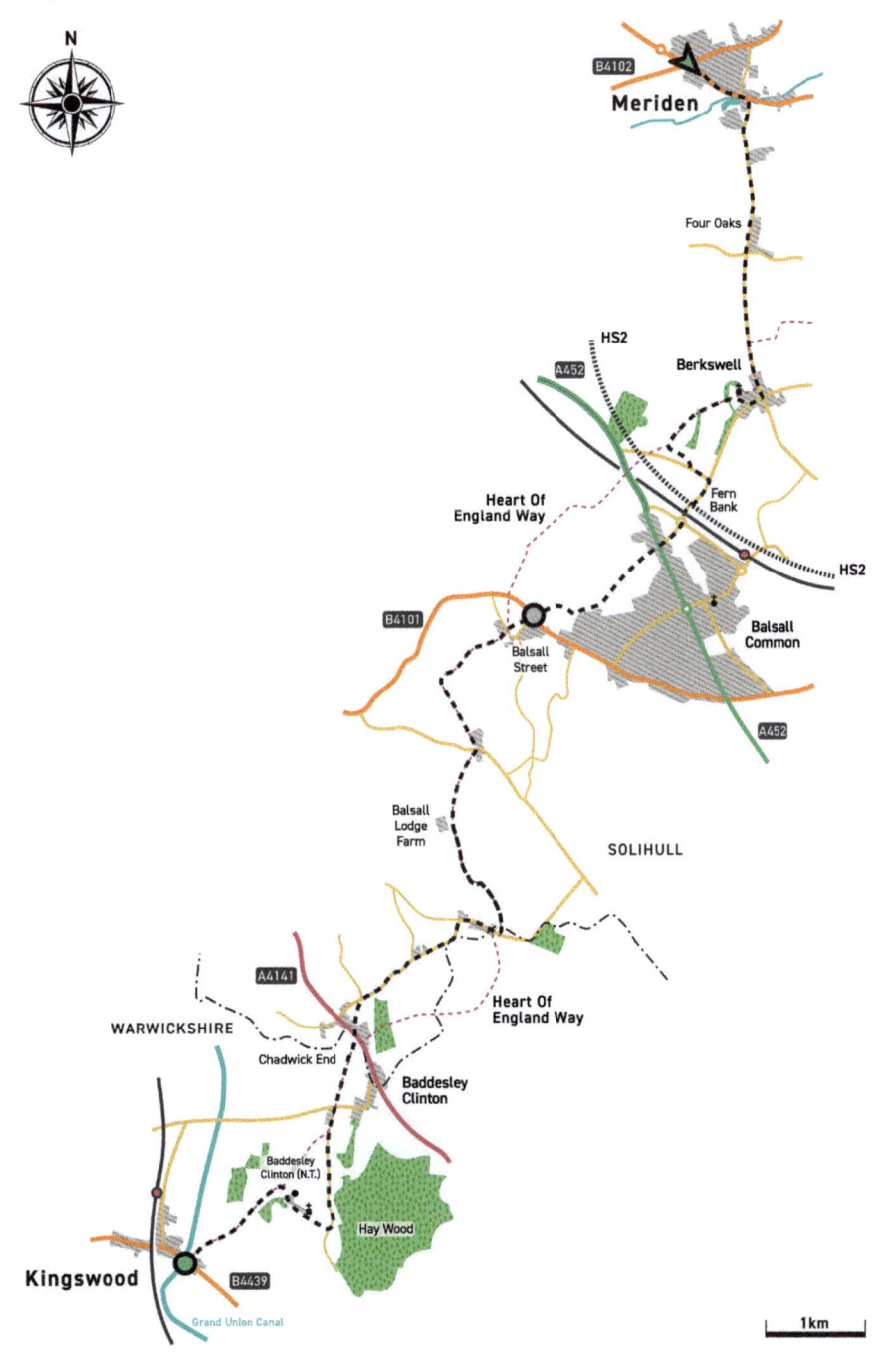

101

After taking my life into my own hands on the busy road, I reached the point where the Heart of England Way came in from the left just before the village of Berkswell. Sauntering into the centre of the village, I sat for a while at the crossroads by the village noticeboard. I turned significantly west at the crossroads which marks the furthest easterly point on this perambulation around the West Midlands. I observed a small village green with mature trees and integral wooden stocks surrounded by traditional rural cottages. I wondered whether the stocks were ever used for summer party games. There was a small village school and a muddy hollow which was the well that gives the village its name. The main axis of this splendid, unspoilt former Warwickshire village, now part of Solihull, was on the east/west lane. Strolling on past the large church into the churchyard, I got into conversation with a local chap out for his morning exercise, who had been decanted out from Chelmsley Wood by the local authority. He directed me onwards but warned me that the way was brutally blocked further on by the HS2 construction works. We both agreed that the continual noise from motorways was much more intrusive than any intermittent noise from an electric railway.

Berkswell Church © AJD

Leaving the church precinct, I walked on through low, wet fields where the path had been set up on a wooden walkway. I was relieved to be off road surfaces that had been my fate for the last eight miles or so since Shustoke. To my right across grazed fields, sitting on top of its mound, was the local grand hall set within parkland, containing lakes created from another dammed stream running down to the River Blythe. Further on, ignoring a sign instructing pedestrians to go to the right, because I didn't want to be diverted to the right, I pressed along the Heart of England Way. I carried on relentlessly along a rising field margin to come slap bang into a metal fence, barring the way as predicted. I wondered about the legal position in actually blocking a designated long-distance footpath in this way. Working my way south-eastwards beside this barrier I observed massive earth-moving machinery reshaping the landscape in anticipation of a new high-speed railway link to the north. Soon, I was able to cut through a strip of woodland, which, from my map, appeared to define the local estate, and gain access to the lane which had been commandeered by the construction works.

I strolled down the lane to the wrong side of the checkpoint, being politely challenged on a number of occasions regarding what my business was in this lane. At the checkpoint at the end of the lane, I was required to explain my progress. It reminded me of an occasion of a field visit to Berlin in 1969 when I was a town planning student at the then Oxford polytechnic. I had gone for an unscheduled evening walk and found myself walking alongside the Berlin Wall. I saw the forbidding watch towers graced by guards with unbelievably powerful weapons. I rambled on, only to come to a road in no man's land between checkpoints for West Berlin and East Germany. I was allowed to pass back into West Berlin, thankfully without too much fuss, even though I didn't know a word of German, to the muted amusement of the guards on duty. Thankfully, at this more modest checkpoint manned by HS2 guards, there were no guns in evidence.

I think now is the right time to pontificate on the relative merits of HS2, given that the scheme is so controversial and there is so much local opposition. In my view, any improvements to the transport network should be generally welcomed. However, the devil is in the detail of implementation. Having decided to build it, I wish that money was spent on the construction phase rather than countless reviews and reports keeping an army of consultants in business. The landscape is always changing through our intervention and, as previously suggested, the noise from a railway is much less than from a motorway. However, in churning through the landscape, considerable damage can be done, and there is rarely sufficient money to carry out the necessary remedial work. This conclusion is based on my experience of walking in Kent and the observed disruption caused by HS1. The sort of actions I have in mind are recreating a network of footpaths and footbridges, reorganising field hedgerows, planting up marginal land adjacent to the track with trees and reconstructing parish boundaries. In effect, instigating a variety of means to allow the landscape to evolve and heal itself. By and large, there is always insufficient money to invest in these measures and, as a consequence, we often end up with rubbish-strewn dead-end lanes and overgrown footpaths. Unfortunately, if the true cost of these measures were calculated at the outset, it would be so vast that the project would never get off the ground in the first place, but at least the futile activity of costing the scheme, followed by frequent hikes in the cost, could be avoided, thus ending this ill-informed rant.

Picking up the lane from Berkswell, I crossed the next railway line at Fern Bank. I came up to a new road, not shown on my map, effectively bypassing Balsall Common and giving direct access to Berkswell Station. The settlement of Balsall Common is mainly a recent twentieth-century development coalescing a number of smaller hamlets. I stood for a while by a bright new roundabout before passing into the Lavender Hill country park. Thereafter, I strolled down Lavender Hill Lane to the north-eastern extremities of Balsall Common strung out in ribbon-development fashion along the A452. Crossing over the road, I followed well-used, local dog walking footpaths, north of Balsall Common. As I approached the back of a peripheral housing estate, and after crossing a small stream, the footpath was barred by a padlocked gate. As a consequence, I skirted around this obstacle and traipsed up along a field edge. Coming to the corner of the field, I climbed through barbed wire that had been broken down by other walkers who had been forced to come this way. Then I passed gingerly through an uneven, overgrown field and came up to the main road, the B4101, just down from Ye Olde Saracen's Head pub in the older hamlet of Balsall Street, which I frequented at exactly one o'clock.

Sitting at a raised table in shouting distance from the bar, I ordered food and drink. I pondered on the pub's name and its reference to the medieval crusades, noting that the nearby village of Temple Balsall was the site of a Templar's hall, a stopover for knights destined for the Holy Land. The Knights Templar were a European Christian military order founded in 1118. The majority of the members of this charity were non-combatants and were concerned with fundraising and established a network of halls across the country. They were disbanded in 1312 by papal decree, partly because they had become so rich and prosperous and partly because of pressure from Philip IV King of France who was able to rescind a massive debt by their abolition. I did wonder whether Christian knights, in all their finery, would have sat and caroused in this very spot where I was sitting, recounting the number of Saracens' heads they had decapitated. After relaxing for an hour or so, I asked the bar staff to order me a taxi. Waiting for another hour in which no taxi

Ye Olde Saracen's Head, Balsall Street © Richard Law

arrived, I was obliged to imbibe in more beer than I had planned. At this point, I gave up on taxis and implored my long-suffering partner to drive out from Birmingham and pick me up. This was the first time on this trip that I was let down by local taxi services.

Returning to Balsall Street in early November on a dank, overcast day, I started out again on another leg, setting off down Magpie Lane, still following the Heart of England Way. This was the first time I had ever walked in November, putting this experience entirely down to the warming effects of climate change. I descended to a small stream feeding the River Blythe and realised, due to the soggy conditions on the path, that my feet were going to get rather wet. This was due to the unfortunate fact that my walking boots, worn out by many miles of trekking, had developed lesions in both soles. I also realised that, although not crossing this significant river, I had been travelling southwards on the eastern side of the River Blythe, crossing many small tributaries in the process, since Shustoke Reservoir.

I strolled on through the rolling Warwickshire countryside, through fields sown with winter wheat, to the drone of planes sinking down to the airport. There was also some sheep and fields of beet with ancient oak trees dotted around. I plodded on along concrete slatted track past a sparkling pond associated with Balsall Lodge Farm. When I came to the next lane, the long-distance footpath was diverted around a massive field, because it was, according to a notice on the stile in the hedge, growing a special type of wheat, and so I elected to take the lane to Chadwick End instead. Nearing this hamlet on the A4141 (which used to be the A40 before it was reclassified), I took a shortcut across fields to emerge in front of the Orange Tree public house where I paused for a while to assess my situation.

It was too early for a proper break, so I pressed on southwards on the designated footpath, bypassing the village of Baddesley Clinton. After the next lane junction, I carried on looking for the footpath off the lane to the right. Although I studied the hedgerow carefully, I found no such path, and so I carried on down the lane past Hay Wood, a Forestry Commission open-access wood, to find a short path to Baddesley Clinton Church. Like many churches marooned in the countryside, there was not much going on, except an infrequent, no doubt badly attended, service. I passed in front of Baddesley Clinton Manor House and decided to have another gander, using my National Trust membership card. This splendid thirteenth-century medieval moated manor house, formally set in the heart of the Forest of Arden, is famous for its hidden priest holes installed by its Catholic owners in the sixteenth century, in common with many other houses in the Midlands during the protestant reformation. Setting off down the drive, I picked up the Heart of England Way again through sheep-ravaged fields. I pressed on across a small stream and through the so-called Kingswood Park, a serious equestrian enterprise, of which there are a number of such examples in the countryside to the south of the conurbation. At this point I was to finally depart from the Heart of England Way that I had been intermittently following since I first reached the erratic Boulder on Cannock Chase.

Thus, arriving in Kingswood, and coming up to the Old Warwick Road, I elected to sojourn in The Navigation Inn, on the side of the

Baddesley Clinton House from the west © David Gearing

Grand Union Canal. I entered by the perfect front room and made myself comfortable, ordering food and drink from the modest bar. I enjoyed the whole experience except that the edge was taken off it by the playing of mindless Christmas records. I sat out for an hour or so, relaxing, reflecting, before ordering a taxi to take me back to Kings Heath in the suburbs of Britain's second city. I say this with a certain degree of tongue in cheek, because it is quite an amazing fact that Birmingham, my adopted city, has achieved this status, growing from a small hamlet to a burgeoning metropolis in the years since the industrial revolution.

Returning after a few days, I pressed on around the southern flank of the conurbation. For the rest of my journey, I was able to consult a more detailed map, Explorer 220. Setting off from The Navigation Inn, on a bright dry day in November, I turned significantly westwards, aiming initially for the old village of Lapworth. However, the whole vicinity is referred to as Lapworth, as indeed is the nearby main line station, although the immediate area based around the canal junction of the Grand Union and Stratford-upon-Avon is known as Kingswood. Lapworth itself, as I was to find out, is no more than a hamlet with an impressive church and a scattering of elegant dwellings away to the west. This major canal junction gives rise to some attractive balancing lakes hard by the road and a delightful flight of locks raising the Stratford-upon-Avon Canal onto the Midland plateau, leading away to the west.

Getting my act together, I strode out along the towpath and after the top lock by Lapworth Farm, I came back to the Old Warwick Road. In crossing over the road, and finding the footpath to Lapworth village, I was swamped by a group of thirty-odd ramblers out from Coventry. I let them pass on their relentless quest and ambled on behind. One of the passing ladies likened my visage to that of Bill Oddie, but much as I could be flattered by the comparison, I have to say I can't see it myself. I trekked on across the fields, and over stiles, to come to the immaculate spectacle of the lovingly manicured grounds of Lapworth Cricket Club, an inspiring sight indeed. Crossing over Tapster Lane, and after further chat with the Coventry ramblers, I pressed on to

TAMWORTH TO ALVECHURCH

Map 17: Kingswood to Tanworth

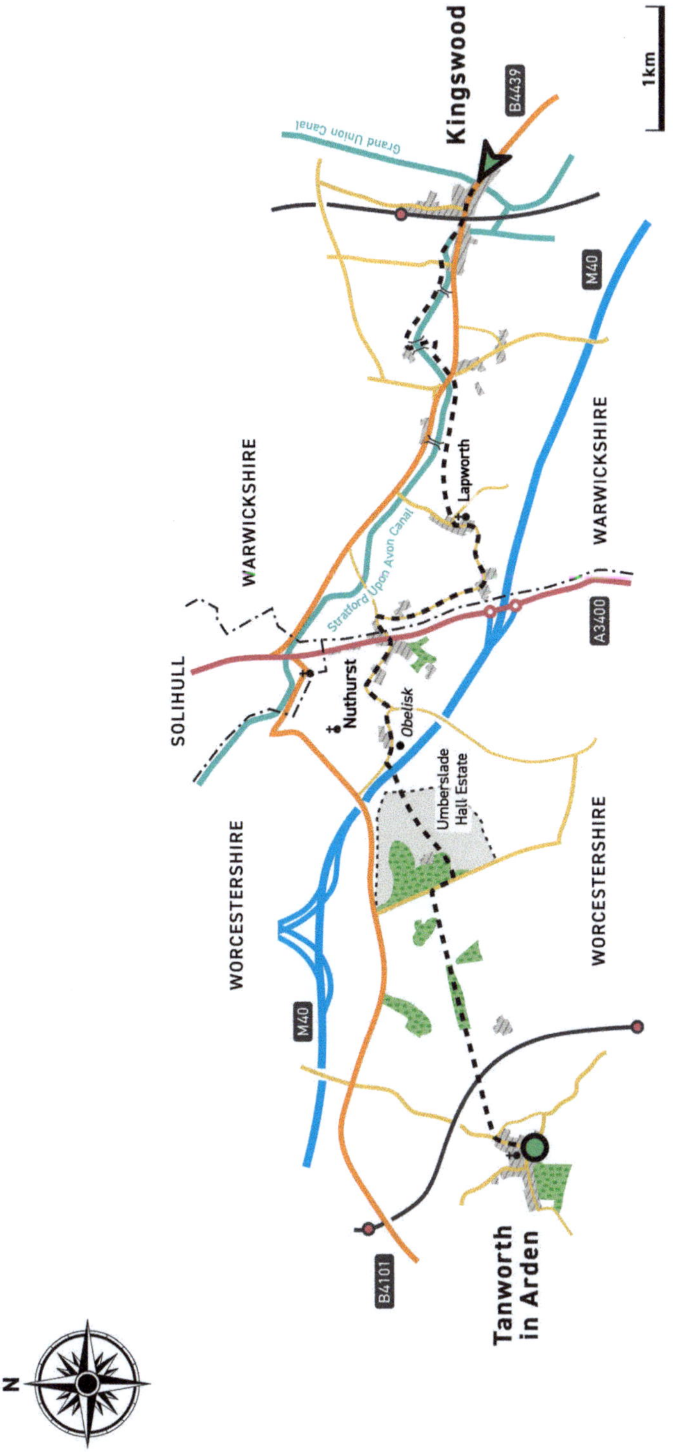

the impressive Lapworth church. The ramblers were draped around the entrance to this evidently notable church, and so, not wishing to get involved in any discussion of the religious significance of the interior, I carried on to the next lane. I stood for a while and gazed around, observing some very pleasant houses in this small village off the beaten track. Later, researching at home, I felt it a curiosity that Lapworth village is located on the western edge of the parish rather than more centrally and includes the more, already passed through, substantial settlement of Kingswood. The M40 slices the parish into two halves with very little connectivity between the northern and southern parts, consisting only of a couple of footbridges over the M42. I carried on along a well-worn path over a bluff down to a small stream. Looking back, I could see the disembodied church spire striking an elegant pose, like an exclamation mark, above the grassy bank.

Evidently, I was now walking on the Millennium Way again, according to a circular disk on the bridge over the stream. Later, I discovered that the Millennium Way was a hundred-mile long-distance footpath with forty-four circular walks, starting in Pershore and ending up in Banbury after peaking in Meriden, created presumably in the year 2000. Thus, I'm not surprised that I encountered this walk on a number of occasions, because part of the route mirrors my own journey and one of the circular walks is based on Lapworth and Kingswood. I pressed on to the next lane and turned northwards for a while along Spring Lane. There was a footpath opposite Lapworth Farm which I declined to use since it was badly overgrown and inaccessible. Instead, I pressed on to Wharf Lane where I turned westwards again and came up to the A3400, the Stratford

View of Lapworth Church spire

Road, which I crossed with care, taking the small lane nearly opposite to Nuthurst. I sauntered down wet lanes, past the entrance to Nuthurst Grange and on to Obelisk Farm. There is no real village of Nuthurst on the ground, even though it is an ancient manor mentioned in the *Domesday Book*, an historical record instituted by William the Conqueror in 1086. Maybe there are some undiscovered lumps and bumps in a nearby field, the site, perhaps, of a lost medieval village, waiting to be discovered. I took a footpath past the striking obelisk to find the tunnel under the M40 motorway. This obelisk, properly called the Umberslade Obelisk, is associated with Umberslade Hall, from where it can be seen, presumably enhancing the view from that stately pile. It is now sliced off from the main part of the estate by the M42 motorway.

Umberslade Obelisk © David P. Howard

Crossing under the motorway, I waded through wet fields to climb up into the landscaped, now neglected and much-reduced estate grounds of Umberslade Hall. The massive and magnificent redwood trees dotted around in the park were a testament to its former glory. I slogged up beside a field boundary which separated the main inner grounds from the peripheral grounds given over to rough sheep pasture. I came up to the lane called the Nuthurst Road and turned right for a short distance to stand at the front entrance to the grand hall. At this high point of 146 metres, I could still hear the hum of the nearby motorway. The manor of Umberslade dates back to the twelfth century when Henry II granted it to the Archer family who held it for six hundred years. Later descendants replaced the old hall with the current mansion by 1700, which is now a grade II listed building.

More recently, it has been the home of local MPs and commercial headquarters, before being converted to residential apartments in 1978. I noted that a number of these supposedly grand apartments were now up for sale.

Turning round, I was faced with the mile-plus-long trek along the dead-straight drive through Umberslade Park to the village of Tanworth-in-Arden. A little way down, just past two monumental columns, I paused in my headlong rush and observed fabulous views across the Warwickshire countryside to the south. I settled into a steady walking rhythm, pacing along this long, straight stretch. Passing the entrance to the children's farm, and under an elegant railway arch, I slogged up to a gated entrance on the next lane. From this point looking back, it is a two-mile dead-straight line, through Umberslade Hall, back to the distant obelisk.

I strolled triumphantly into the attractive village, the first of any note since Berkswell, the most southerly point in this circumnavigation of the conurbation. I strolled past the village school, in the heavily parked-up road, to sojourn in The Bell Inn opposite the parish church and facing onto a quaint village green. I met a fellow walker on the threshold of the pub, with whom I swapped stories. He was resting after a local circular walk, but I couldn't help burdening him with my own mammoth efforts now speedily coming to a close. I relaxed in the pub, eating and drinking, before catching a taxi back into Birmingham.

Setting off again a few days later, in amazingly settled weather in mid-November, I started on the last leg of my perambulation around the West Midlands. From Tanworth, actually a hilltop village, I plunged down the slope to cross the headwaters of the River Alne, which flows south to Henley in Arden. I climbed up again to the B4101, past large properties with manicured lawns, demonstrating the affluence of their owners. This settlement pattern stretching from Wood End to Apsley Heath has easy access to the nearby railway station, affording easy commuting into Birmingham. Then I took Penn Lane on the way to Portway. I passed the entrance to Ladbrook Hall on the way to the A435 where I crossed the county boundary from Warwickshire into Worcestershire.

Tanworth-in-Arden © Ian Rob

Arriving in the disorganised hamlet of Portway, I turned north for a short stretch on the now bypassed Alcester Road. This is the place where Mike Hailwood, one of the greatest motorcycle racers of all time, and a Formula One driver, was killed in a road traffic accident in 1981. My lasting impression was of an area given over to extensive car repair and sale premises, scrapyards and old, worn-out industrial units. I located the bridleway I was searching for which emanated from another scruffy, dubious-looking vehicle repair facility, where my transit was eyed with considerable suspicion. Striding past the back of a decaying industrial premises, I made off along the bridleway towards Hob Hill.

At a sharp bend in Billesley Lane, I took the next footpath across flat terrain to Seafield Lane. Directly opposite, the footpath continued as it was diverted away from the affluent-looking Hob Hill Farm, ushering me around the back of this farm complex which housed a horse training centre. After a brief encounter with some lovely

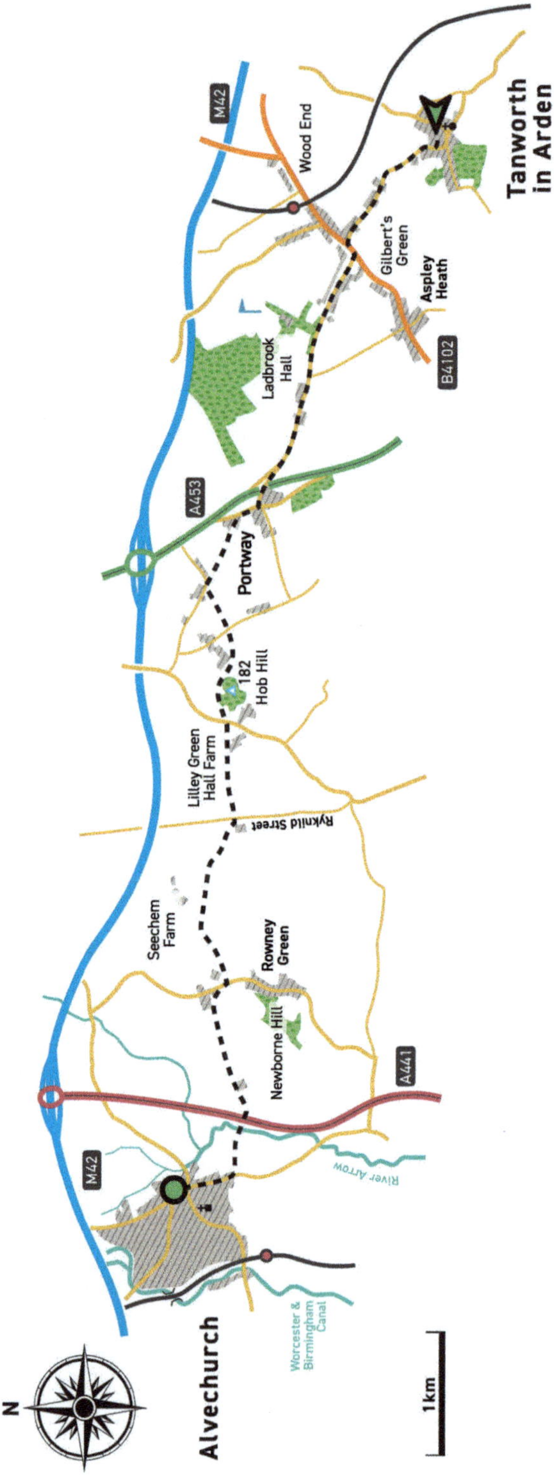

A MIDLAND MEANDER

Map 18: Tanworth to Alvechurch

tame horses in a large training shed who plodded over for a stroke, I pressed on across wet, grassy fields to Hob Hill. This significant hill at 182 metres is part of a distinct escarpment, a landscape feature that runs north-west to south-east, from Wast Hills and Weatheroak Hill to Gorcott Hill on the A435 east of Redditch. I stood for a while at the brow of the hill, admiring the panoramic view northwards towards Birmingham. The chequered landscape of small hedgerowed fields given over to pasture is typical of this part of rural England. In the distance, I could see the Clent and Lickey Hills, a continuation of the same uplifted edge of the Midland plateau. I could see the M42 snaking across the landscape below, with moving traffic shuffling along like a line of industrious ants.

Looking westwards, the land fell away to a hummocky glaciated landscape of small hills carved out by small streams forming the headwaters of the Dagnell Brook joining the River Arrow to the north of Redditch. I was in fact entering, what I have previously called, the Alvechurch bowl, framed by the ridge mentioned above and formed by the River Arrow, which flows south to join the River Alne in Alcester before flowing to the River Avon at Bidford. Thus, the Wast Hills/Gorcott Hill ridge forms a distinct watershed with the waters to the west and south, flowing to the Severn, and the waters to the east and north, as near as Baddesley Clinton, flowing via the River Blythe to the Tame, Trent and eventually the Humber Estuary. Also, Solihull and much of south Birmingham drains out to the River Trent via the River Cole. The Chinn Brook, a tributary of the River Cole, flows yards away from where I live in Brandwood, Kings Heath. In the near distance, in the direction of my travel, was the Rowney Green ridge, a terminal moraine dumped by the retreating ice, and beyond, in the next valley, was my final destination, Alvechurch.

Clambering down the steep slope to the next lane, I felt like bursting exuberantly into song, realising this epic journey was nearly over. I pressed on past a messy farm complex festooned with redundant farm machinery, old tractors and rotting caravans. I always wonder, in farm backwaters like this, tucked away in redundant sheds, why the metal is not recycled; it must be worth a fortune. In contrast, the landscape hereabouts is dominated by pasture with neatly cut hedgerows, demonstrating a well-cared-for farm. However, I always wonder whether such tidiness is not misplaced, given that it severely limits the potential of these hedges as a wildlife habitat. I came down to Ickneild Street, one of the few Roman roads in this area, down in the valley bottom. This long Roman track actually runs from Bourton-on-the-Water in the Cotswolds all the way to South Yorkshire. Locally, it runs from Alcester, a Roman town, through Studley, Redditch and Birmingham to Lichfield, skirting the western edge of the ancient Forest of Arden. There are few Roman settlements across the Midland plateau, except the odd roadside fort such as Metchley near the Queen Elizabeth Hospital in Birmingham. Along with the Forest of Arden, the Midland plateau would have been heavily wooded in Roman times, and the absence of any major settlements may be testament to the proposition that the legions were keen to get through this formally inhospitable area as quickly as possible.

Climbing again, out of the valley to a height of 156 metres, I passed south of Seechem Farm, the successor to a medieval manor house. I passed by another discarded tractor rusting away and took a well-worn footpath, no doubt created by parties of weekend ramblers out from the city. At the rear of the Seechem Equestrian Centre, there were many horse-dominated paddocks, a common enterprise in these parts. Approaching Rowney Green Lane, at the entrance to Rowney Green House Farm, there was, what I believe to be, a magnificent multi-stemmed evergreen oak tree. I stood for a while, admiring its stature, hoping that it was properly protected. I concluded that this Mediterranean species must have been planted since it only self-seeds in the south of England. After a short dog-leg down the lane, I strolled on through the gently undulating countryside, full of sheep around here, on the same well-worn footpath to Alvechurch Lodge Farm. Thereafter, I plunged under the A441, the Alvechurch bypass, through a shady tunnel. Next, I came to the deeply incised stream of the main river hereabouts, that is the River Arrow. Resting for a while, I leant on the bridge parapet and reflected on the fact that this last stage of my journey had been almost entirely on bridleways, probably my favourite surface for rambling. I carried on across Lye meadows to enter the southern extremities of the ancient village of Alvechurch.

I strolled down into the centre of the village on raised pavements, protecting pleasant old cottages and newer dwellings tastefully designed and located in the street scene. This large village, with a population of 5,316, expanded rapidly in the twentieth century with the land between the main road and the Worcester and Birmingham Canal being infilled. It is an ancient settlement, being mentioned in the *Domesday Book*, and in medieval times, the Bishop of Worcester built a palace here on the banks of the River Arrow, but now, only a yew tree and moat survive. I popped into the first pub, The Crown Inn, for the first pint of the day. The landlord, rather too forcefully, informed me that I didn't need to wear a mask when moving around, to which I replied, to his obvious irritation, that it was my preference. Leaving this slightly awkward encounter, I strolled triumphantly through the heart of the village to The Red Lion Inn, the starting point of this epic journey, taking more than two years to complete. I ate and drank liberally, sharing my excitement with an attentive barmaid, before catching a taxi back into Birmingham.

Alvechurch

> *Nestling in a bowl*
> *Ancient palace*
> *By the River Arrow*
> *Only a trace*
> *Now, just a yew tree and a moat.*

Thus ended this 150-mile perambulation around the West Midlands conurbation which I started in the autumn of 2019, before the Covid-19 crisis necessarily slowed down progress. It is difficult to sum up one's feelings after completing such a challenge – is it relief that the relentless effort and commitment is over, or is

The Red Lion, Alvechurch © Stephen McKay

it sadness, not knowing where the next challenge will come from? Sometimes, sitting quietly in my study or leaning on my spade on my allotment, I wonder whether I could walk from Birmingham back to London and Romney Marsh on the Kent coast. Readers who have read my first four books will understand my attachment to that splendid part of our country. Maybe my feelings are best summed up by my favourite poem of Edward Thomas entitled 'Over the Hills' and referred to in the introduction to this narrative. The following lines seem most appropriate.

> …I did not know my loss
> Till one day twelve months later suddenly
> I leaned upon my spade and saw it all,
> Though far beyond the sky-line. It became
> Almost a habit through the year for me
> To lean and see it and think to do the same
> Again for two days and a night…

But, at my advanced, and ever-advancing, age, I doubt whether such an enterprise is viable. Maybe I'll join a local rambling group instead and bore them with my walking exploits carried out over the last twenty-odd years.

Appendix 1
Pubs Visited

Chapter 1
The Red Lion, Alvechurch
Ye Old Black Cross, Bromsgrove
The Red Lion, Bromsgrove
The Queens Head, Bromsgrove
The Chequers, Bromsgrove
The White Hart, Hartlebury
The Angel Inn, Stourport
The Wheatsheaf, Stourport
The Mug House Inn, Bewdley
The Bellmans Cross Inn, Bellmans Cross
The Black Boy Inn, Bewdley
The Fox Inn, Stourton

Chapter 2
The Red Lion, Bobbington
The Crown Inn, Claverley
The Boycott Arms, Upper Ludstone
The Crown Inn, Pattingham
The Pigot Arms, Pattingham

The Red Lion Hotel, Brewood
The Summerhouse, A464 road
The Sun Inn, Brewood

Chapter 3
The Littleton Arms, Penkridge
The Rag Country Inn, Rawnsley
The Globe Inn, Tamworth
The Red Lion, Hopwas

Chapter 4
The Dog and Doublet, Bodymoor Heath
The Bulls Head, Meriden
The Plough, Shustoke
Ye Olde Saracen's Head, Balsall Street
The Navigation Inn, Kingswood
The Bell Inn, Tanworth
The Crown Inn, Alvechurch
The Red Lion, Alvechurch

Appendix 2
Long-Distance Footpaths Trodden

Monarch's Way
Severn Way
Worcestershire Way
Staffordshire Way
Heart of England Way
Centenary Way
Millennium Way

Appendix 3
Canals Encountered

Worcester & Birmingham Canal
Staffordshire & Worcestershire Canal
Shropshire Union Canal
Lichfield Canal (disused)
Coventry Canal
Birmingham & Fazeley Canal
Grand Union Canal
Stratford-upon-Avon Canal

Copyright Acknowledgements

Chapter 1: Alvechurch to Kinver

Alvechurch: Junction of Bear Hill & Red Lion Street
Copyright: Lee J. Andrews. Geograph: 583689
Tardebigge Top Lock
Copyright: Rudi Winter. Geograph 6110830
Bromsgrove: Statue of A. E. Housman
Copyright: Philip Halling. Geograph: 5757245
Hartlebury Church
Copyright: Philip Halling. Geograph: 2550728
The Angel Inn, Stourport
Copyright: Roger Kidd. Geograph: 4763580
The Tontine, Stourport
Copyright: Philip Pankhurst. Geograph: 6095405
Hartlebury Common
Copyright: Richard Greenwood. Geograph: 1173539
The River Severn at Bewdley
Copyright: Matt Fascione. Geograph: 6545735
Holy Austin rock houses near Kinver in Staffordshire
Copyright: Roger Kidd. Geograph: 6661652

Chapter 2: Kinver to Brewood

The Red Lion Inn at Bobbington
Copyright: Roger Kidd. Geograph: 2108767
Scoreboard at Enville Cricket Club
Copyright: John M. Geograph: 2358709

COPYRIGHT ACKNOWLEDGEMENTS

The A458 at Enville
Copyright: P. L. Chadwick. Geograph: 2001812
The Crown – entrance to car park, Claverley high street
Copyright: P. L. Chadwick. Geograph: 6547194
Bull Ring, Lychgate, Claverley
Copyright: Gordan Griffiths. Geograph: 3085834
The Boycott Arms at Upper Ludstone
Copyright: Roger Kidd. Geograph: 4843985
Animal pound at Rudge
Copyright: John M. Geograph: 3741814
The Pigot Arms, Pattingham
Copyright: Philip Halling. Geograph: 5163192
Marketplace in Brewood
Copyright: Roger Kidd. Geograph: 5823707
Avenue Bridge No.10
Copyright: Matt Fascione. Geograph: 5749141
11. The Royal Oak, Boscobel
Copyright: Philip Halling. Geograph: 4994433

Chapter 3: Brewood to Tamworth

Cuttlestone Bridge
Copyright: John M. Geograph: 4910711
Katyn Memorial, Cannock Chase
Copyright: Tricia Neal. Geograph: 3966317
Minster Pool, Lichfield
Copyright: Derek Voller. Geograph: 3727470
Canal at Fazeley Junction in Staffordshire
Copyright: Roger Kidd. Geograph: 6347333
The Red Lion, Hopwas
Copyright: Alan Murray-Rust. Geograph: 4031989
Lady Bridge, Tamworth
Copyright: Humphrey Bolton. Geograph: 1740804

Chapter 4: Tamworth to Alvechurch

Tamworth Castle from Lady Bridge
Copyright: Martin Richard Phelan. Geograph: 6372422
Fazeley Junction
Copyright: Rob Farrow. Geograph: 703609
Drayton footbridge, Drayton Bassett, Staffordshire
Copyright: Roger Kidd. Geograph: 1748099

Cyclists War Memorial, Meriden
Copyright: Keith Williams. Geograph: 852058
Berkswell Church
Copyright: AJD. Geograph: 6137457
Ye Olde Saracen's Head, Balsall Street
Copyright: Richard Law. Geograph: 5534971
Baddesley Clinton House from the west
Copyright: David Gearing. Geograph: 6195271
Umberslade Obelisk
Copyright: David P. Howard. Geograph: 3228488
Tanworth-in-Arden
Copyright: Ian Rob. Geograph: 5288551
The Red Lion, Alvechurch
Copyright: Stephen McKay. Geograph: 6927277

This book is printed on paper from sustainable sources managed under the Forest Stewardship Council (FSC) scheme.

It has been printed in the UK to reduce transportation miles and their impact upon the environment.

For every new title that The Book Guild publishes, we plant a tree to offset CO_2, partnering with the More Trees scheme.

MORE TREES
LET'S PLANT A BILLION TREES

For more about how The Book Guild offsets its environmental impact, see www.bookguild.co.uk